"I wish I could have read this book in ministry. Jason's writing is mark and the sure-footed wisdom that o. This personal, practical volume will serve as a valuable guide for many young pastors, and quite a few older ones too."

Kevin DeYoung, senior pastor of University Reformed Church; author of *Crazy Busy: A (Mercifully) Short Book about a (Really) Big Problem*

"The joys of pastoral ministry are enormous, but so are the challenges. Helopoulos's work is a welcome guide for new pastors as they confront the many difficult issues new pastors regularly face. New pastors and their churches will be greatly served by this book."

R. Albert Mohler Jr., president of Southern Baptist Theological Seminary

"I wish *The New Pastor's Handbook* had been available when I was starting out. Thirty-nine years on, it is a helpful reminder to do the basics. I commend it enthusiastically."

Alistair Begg, senior pastor of Parkside Church

"If you are sensing a call to ministry or in the early years of ministry, this book is a must read. As a pastor for over thirty years, I find Jason's book has reenergized my own calling. May God use it as a template for gospel training."

Bob Bouwer, senior pastor of Faith Church (RCA)

"Finally, a practical and thorough guide for real pastors in the trenches of real ministry. This book tells you what they don't tell you in seminary. I have been in some form of ministry for twenty years now, and this is precisely the sort of book I could have used at the outset of my service to the church. Pastor

Helopoulos shows us how we are to be not only shepherds of God's flock but also, more fundamentally, shepherds of our own hearts and homes. I want to get this into the hands of every seminary student and every new pastor to the end that Jesus Christ might be glorified in our love and care of his bride."

Burk Parsons, copastor of Saint Andrew's Chapel;
editor of *Tabletalk* magazine

"Jason Helopoulos has written a modern classic that will prove to be as helpful as *The Christian Ministry* by Charles Bridges has been since 1830. Every new or young pastor should consider this required reading as they follow God's call in their life to serve the church."

Joe Thorn, lead pastor of Redeemer Fellowship

"So who is helping younger pastors these days, especially in their first church? It is hard to come up with a name or two. Well, you can add Jason Helopoulos to the list. Jason has a burden to reach out and help younger pastors, and he can help you too in *The New Pastor's Handbook*."

Aubrey Malphurs, professor of leadership
and pastoral ministries at Dallas Theological Seminary;
founder of the Malphurs Group

"Where was this book when I was first ordained? *The New Pastor's Handbook* is the perfect book to give to a new pastor (or an old one, for that!). Ultrapractical and stuffed full of timeless wisdom, this is a book I will recommend often and reread regularly."

Tim Challies, author of *The Next Story*;
pastor of Grace Fellowship Church

The NEW PASTOR'S HANDBOOK

HELP AND ENCOURAGEMENT FOR THE FIRST YEARS OF MINISTRY

JASON HELOPOULOS

Foreword by Ligon Duncan

BakerBooks

a division of Baker Publishing Group
Grand Rapids, Michigan

Published by Baker Books
a division of Baker Publishing Group
P.O. Box 6287, Grand Rapids, MI 49516-6287
www.bakerbooks.com

Printed in the United States of America

Library of Congress Cataloging-in-Publication Data
Helopoulos, Jason.
    The new pastor's handbook : help and encouragement for the first years
of ministry / Jason Helopoulos.
        pages cm
    Includes bibliographical references.
    ISBN 978-0-8010-1835-0 (pbk.)
    1. Pastoral theology. I. Title.
    BV4011.3.H45 2015
    253—dc23   2015015861

15   16   17   18   19   20   21   7   6   5   4   3   2

To Paul Settle, Ligon Duncan, Thomas Watson,
John Calvin, Richard Baxter, and Jonathan Edwards—
faithful pastors who have shaped and informed
my own pastoring in significant ways.

Contents

Contents

Part 3 Encouragements

Contents

Contents

Foreword

The apostle Paul once wrote to a young pastor and said, "Do your best to present yourself to God as one approved, a worker who has no need to be ashamed, rightly handling the word of truth" (2 Tim. 2:15). In fact, Paul's letters are filled with those kinds of exhortations, specifically intended for those starting out in ministry.

Train yourself for godliness. (1 Tim. 4:7)

Let no one despise you for your youth, but set the believers an example in speech, in conduct, in love, in faith, in purity. (1 Tim. 4:12)

So flee youthful passions and pursue righteousness, faith, love, and peace, along with those who call on the Lord from a pure heart. Have nothing to do with foolish, ignorant controversies; you know that they breed quarrels. And the Lord's servant must not be quarrelsome but kind to everyone, able to teach, patiently enduring evil, correcting his opponents with gentleness. God may perhaps grant them repentance leading to a knowledge of the truth, and they may come to their senses and escape from the snare of the devil, after being captured by him to do his will. (2 Tim. 2:22–26)

The list could go on. The point is, Paul is deliberate and specific in providing exhortation and encouragement to a new pastor (who, in this case, is his beloved son in the Lord, Timothy) at the outset of his ministry, and Paul's words, being by the inspiration of the Holy Spirit, also guide our investment in and preparation of young pastors, in every age. Paul gave that help and encouragement because Timothy needed that help and encouragement. And so do new pastors in every age.

That is why Jason Helopoulos wrote *The New Pastor's Handbook: Help and Encouragement for the First Years of Ministry.* In it he engages the reader in a conversation that is not only useful in the early years of ministry but also sets the stage for long-term faithfulness and fruitfulness. The considerations here—the issues, circumstances, challenges, and, importantly, delights of ministry—are all important to think through at the outset of ministry. Those currently training for the ministry, or just starting out as an assistant pastor, or in the first years of a church plant, or in their first church as a solo minister, or beginning a pastorate in a new place (to mention no more) will all find the discussion here helpful. Additionally, Jason provides seasoned pastors with a good outline of issues to think through as they mentor and encourage seminarians and young ministers. I am personally thankful for that particular application of the book.

Jason Helopoulos is one of a new generation of pastors who deeply encourages me. I have known him since he was a young ministerial candidate in Dallas, Texas, and I have followed his service of the Lord and his church with gratitude ever since those days. You will quickly discover that, though he is not as young as he used to be, he is still wise beyond his years. You will also find that the topics that he addresses here are very pertinent to and timely for those who are just starting out in ministry (I should also say that veteran pastors will be edified, as I was, in reading this book). The chapters are brief and the topics wide ranging. In the midst of much practical wisdom, forthright consideration of problems, and counsel on dangers and priorities, I love the note of hope and joy that Jason strikes. He calls us to perseverance, to endurance in the pastoral ministry, because he knows its value and its end. He is fully aware of its challenges, and he understands there are pitfalls, but he also knows the blessing, glory, and gladness of serving God and his people. The biblical and prudential wisdom here serves a number of functions: to set our expectations so that when disappointments come, we are neither surprised nor unduly discouraged; to prime us so that when decisions have to be made, we have thought about them ahead of time; to prepare and equip us for the long haul in ministry; and to call us to a deliberate self-awareness.

In Acts 20:28, in his final earthly meeting with the Ephesian elders, the apostle Paul exhorted them to "be on guard for yourselves and for all the flock, among which the Holy Spirit has made you overseers, to shepherd the church of God which He purchased with His own blood" (NASB). That urgent challenge—to shepherd the flock of God, the church of God, the very people of God, bought at an unfathomable cost—has rung in the heart of every faithful Christian pastor ever since, bringing both inspiration and conviction. Paul is setting before us the pastoral task, building in us an aspiration to it, and specifically urging us to undertake it faithfully. We all need that.

Paul says three things: as pastors-elders-shepherds-leaders, (1) watch over yourselves; (2) guide, direct, protect, feed, and help the flock of God; and (3) remember what they cost God and how valuable they are to him.

Don't miss Paul's astounding third point: pastors-elders-shepherds-leaders have been entrusted with God's own inheritance, purchased with the blood of his Son. That is, Paul reminds us of the exceeding preciousness of the people whom he has called us to pastor. Listen again to how he says it: they are "the church of God which He purchased with His own blood." This reminds us that in being called to shepherd God's flock we are being called to care for something of staggering value to God.

God himself has redeemed, purchased, and paid for his people, his church, his vineyard, his Son's body, his children. This has been done through the infinite cost of the death and dereliction of his own Son. Surely it is a grave thing to be entrusted with such a gift. God has entrusted to you his own children, the blood-bought brothers and sisters of Jesus Christ, and said, "Tell them what I'm like. Give them my good news. Proclaim my grace. Keep the wolves away from them. Teach them to trust in my Son Jesus, to love my Word. Show them how to glorify me in all of life. And prepare them to be with me forever."

Young pastors and those preparing for the ministry, you must realize the exceeding preciousness to God of what he has given or is giving into your arms and prepare accordingly. Jason's wise counsel is here to help you to that end.

Ligon Duncan

Chancellor and CEO of Reformed Theological Seminary

John E. Richards Professor of Systematic and Historical Theology

Acknowledgments

There are many who made this book possible. I am thankful for Baker Books and especially Brian Vos for the opportunity to publish this work.

Kevin DeYoung's early encouragement was key in this book seeing the light of day. He is a pastor from whom I have learned a great deal, and I am thankful to count him as my dear friend.

Much of the content of this volume is the result of watching older and wiser pastors who set good examples before me. While they are too many to list, their impact has been significant.

I am thankful for Rob Allen, Ron Williams, Roger Wiles, Robby Rucker, and Paul Settle, all seasoned men in ministry, who intentionally spent time mentoring a twenty-something, zealous, overconfident young man. They sowed many of the seeds of wisdom and practical advice that are present in this book.

As always, thank you to my dear wife, Leah, who has been a true helpmate in the midst of this ministerial journey. She is a faithful friend, wiser than I shall ever be. I am a better pastor with her by my side. Thank you also to my two children, Gracen and Ethan, who fill me with delight and encouraged me throughout this writing project, routinely asking, "Daddy, how many chapters do you have left to write now?"

Most importantly, I want to thank the congregations that have afforded me the privilege to serve as their pastor: Meadow-view Reformed Presbyterian Church, Christ Church, Providence Presbyterian, and University Reformed Church. Much of the content of this book was learned by way of experience—and not always by taking the easiest road. I am grateful for your patience and long-suffering, and for the encouragement you extended to a pastor who needed his fair share of each. It has been my honor to serve alongside you.

Opening Words

A Holy Calling

The diploma reads "Master of Divinity" or "Master of Theology." That first week in the church involves incredible excitement about this new season of life, the call you received, the task placed before you, and the realization of all those years of study. Somewhere in the second or third week you begin to experience a little panic. You come to the jarring conclusion that you are not quite the "Master of Divinity" your diploma says you are. You can exegete from the original languages, critique the best sermons, and wade through the deep waters of the hypostatic union, but you suddenly realize you lack knowledge about a lot of practical things—things you have never done and aren't even sure you know how to do. Seminary didn't teach you everything.

If you are a pastor and find yourself in such a situation, you are in good company. Every pastor before you has traveled this road. My hope is that this book will help you avoid some of the potholes on the journey. It will not make ministry easy or painless. However, it may spare you a little unnecessary trouble, and, maybe more importantly, spare your congregation a little unnecessary trouble too.

A friend asked me why I was writing this book. He wasn't as concerned about the book's subject as he was about me being the author! He said, "You are neither a famous pastor nor a pastor nearing retirement with a lifetime of ministry to look back on, so why you?" No doubt many other pastors could write a better book on this subject. I do not pretend to be an authority on pastoring. Rather, I am an ordinary pastor continuing to grow in the pastorate who loves the church, loves my fellow brothers in the ministry, and passionately desires to help men at the beginning of this glorious calling. I am thankful for the older pastors who came alongside me over the years, equipping me for the challenges of ministry.

In turn, I ask you to consider this book as an outstretched helping hand from a pastor a little further along in the journey than you—a pastor who experienced his first years of ministry just a decade ago. Those memories and challenges are still fresh in my mind. I hope this freshness, along with some seasoning through experience as the years have passed, will provide ready wisdom and aid to those just beginning this journey. Much of this book draws on advice mentors have given me over the years, but some of it is what I wish I had known and unfortunately only learned by experience.

I think of those first months of pastoral ministry and of a wise pastor telling me to move slowly. I was zealous and filled with ideas. Implementing a host of new initiatives in the children's and youth ministries of the church were the first items on my list. However, the parents of these children didn't know me, and I didn't know them, which was a recipe for disaster. Thankfully, this wise pastor's encouragement slowed me down and provided the opportunity to foster trust before making sweeping changes. I think of another seasoned minister who charged me to devote my first couple of years in ministry to learning as much from the Scriptures as I could. He said, "Don't get entangled in controversies early in ministry. Devote your first years to learning the Scriptures above all else." This wonderfully practical advice has provided a strong foundation for all my years as a pastor (this will be discussed in more detail in chap. 9).

I also think of the difficult lessons I learned by experience. Nothing prepared me for the sting of betrayal in the church. I don't remember anyone warning me about this hazard in seminary or during those first couple of years of pastoral ministry, but I've discovered my situation was not unique. I recently spoke at a conference for pastors on this very subject. A young pastor came up to me afterward with tears streaming down his cheeks and said, "I almost left the ministry over this very thing. Betrayal wasn't on my radar." He and his wife were devastated, and we spent twenty minutes talking and praying through his situation. I hope betrayal never happens to you, but it is helpful to be prepared in case it does (this will be discussed in more detail in chap. 40). This book is aimed at such issues—practical advice to aid you as you set out on a lifetime of ministry.

My brothers, we have a high calling. A holy task has been set before us. It isn't always fun. It isn't always easy. It isn't always pleasurable. But I know the vast majority of us can testify that nothing is more rewarding or joy stirring than serving Christ and his dear bride! The Great Shepherd of the sheep has called and equipped us to serve as his undershepherds, those charged with the care of his precious flock. We enjoy one of the great honors and privileges of this life. May the Lord help us to serve his people well, unto his glory. I hope in writing this book to help you live as a more faithful and effective minister of the gospel, even as I join you in this lifelong calling to grow as a pastor. I sit with you at the feet of Christ, pleading, "Teach me, humble me, convict me, and equip me, so I may be a better servant in your church for its good and your glory." Let's march onward.

PART 1

The

BEGINNING

1

What Is a Call?

And he gave the apostles, the prophets, the evangelists, the pastors [ESVmg.] and teachers, to equip the saints for the work of ministry, for building up the body of Christ.

Ephesians 4:11–12

What do we mean when we say someone is "called" to the ministry? *Call* can include many different definitions. A *call* can be a loud voice, a brief visit with a friend, or even a moment in a card game. None of these refers to the *call* of God to vocational ministry.

In the Scriptures we see that Zacchaeus responded to the call of Christ (Luke 19:5–6). In fact, Christ calls every Christian to service in his name (Eph. 4:4). Without that call on our lives we would not be Christians. As Paul says to Timothy, "But share in suffering for the gospel by the power of God, who saved us and called us to a holy calling, not because of our works but because of his own purpose and grace, which he gave us in Christ Jesus before the ages began" (2 Tim. 1:8b–9). To be a Christian is to be called. He summons each of us to holiness and labor for the sake of the kingdom (1 Cor. 10:31).

Yet, it is also true that Christ extends a distinct and particular call to those who serve as pastors of his people. He summons some to a specific office, responsibility, and function in the church. Paul clearly articulates that the church is built on the foundation of the apostles and prophets (Eph. 2:20), and in the centuries to follow, the church has continued its upbuilding through the ministry of evangelists, pastors, and teachers (Eph. 4:11–14).

Pastors possess a distinct calling from others in the body of Christ. However, this does not diminish the need for every other Christian in the body to contribute his or her necessary service. On the contrary, "If the whole body were an eye, where would be the sense of hearing? If the whole body were an ear, where would be the sense of smell? But as it is, God arranged the members in the body, each one of them, as he chose. If we were a single member, where would the body be? As it is, there are many parts, yet one body" (1 Cor. 12:17–20). The church needs each and every one of us. As pastors, we serve as members of the body distinctly called to proclaim, explain, and apply the living Word of God (2 Tim. 4:2). We "equip the saints for the work of the ministry, for building up the body of Christ" (Eph. 4:12).

We have a particular call marked by requisite gifts of the Holy Spirit (1 Cor. 12; Eph. 4; 1 Tim. 4:14). This great service demands sacrificial love (Rom. 9:3), holiness (1 Tim. 3:2–7; 4:12–13), and the pouring out of our lives for the sake of others and the gospel of Jesus Christ (Phil. 2:17). A pastor functions as a counselor, a friend, a guide, and a leader. He will fulfill many roles. He operates as a shepherd and physician of the soul. Above all, he is a man under obligation to proclaim the Word of God with authority, accuracy, and faithfulness (2 Tim. 2:15) for the benefit of the body and the glory of God (2 Tim. 4:2). Did God call you as a pastor? Then this is your high calling. As undershepherds of his great flock, we care for his sheep by feeding them the Word; it is the very core and heartbeat of the calling on our lives.

||||||||||||

2

How Do You Know Whether You Are Called?

The saying is trustworthy: If anyone aspires to the office
of overseer, he desires a noble task.

1 Timothy 3:1

Has God called you to pastoral ministry? Three essential elements help answer this question: internal call, manifest approval by God's people, and the confirmation of the church.

I enrolled at seminary as a unique student. I had no desire to become a pastor. Rather, I entered seminary as a young Christian motivated by a thirst to learn the Bible and theology. It was not until my third year of seminary that I began to wrestle with the call to the pastorate. One particular afternoon, I shared this internal struggle with my wife. We discussed the advice others had given me on the subject. Some friends suggested that if I could do anything else and remain happy, then I wasn't called. If that was the case, then Moses, Jeremiah, Jonah, and a host of other biblical leaders wouldn't have served the Lord as they did. That couldn't be the answer.

Others told me that if I possessed the gifts for ministry then God was clearly calling me. However, this also struck me as inconclusive; I knew many women who were better teachers and leaders than most men, but they weren't called to be pastors (1 Tim. 3:2; Titus 1:6). That couldn't be the answer either.

My wife then asked, "Jason, would you be obedient if you did anything else?" In that moment, I knew that if I chose to do anything else with my life vocationally it would be an act of disobedience against God. You may not experience a particular moment like this. However, any man seeking to enter the ministry should have an internal sense that God has called him to be a pastor (Gal. 1:1; Eph. 1:1). You must feel that burden, that tug of the heart, that nagging, piercing prod from the Lord that he indeed called you to this holy task.

Some will have a stronger sense of calling than others. Don't let this discourage you. Some of us lean more toward introspection, and doubt can quickly enter our minds. Others of us have seemingly always known that God called us to labor as pastors. Whether we doubt or are supremely confident in our internal call, the other two essential elements of discernment are necessary and helpful. For the doubter, the other elements reassure him of the call on his life. For the supremely confident, these elements help by either confirming his certainty or providing the necessary outside voice against his perceived calling.

Simply sensing an internal call does not provide sufficient evidence of God's call on your life. There also must be an external call, which is provided by those within the church (the people of God) and by the church itself (through the offer of a formal call). The people of God must agree that you possess the gifts and biblical qualifications for the ministry (1 Tim. 3; Titus 1). Do those who sit under your teaching, preaching, and leading attest with approval that they see these gifts in you? Have others in the local church benefited from your ministry? Has fruit been borne? The final confirmation comes in the form of the courts of the church (local congregation, elders, presbytery, etc.) who, by extending a formal call to you, confirm that they also believe you possess the gifts and qualifications for a pastor (Acts 15; Titus 1:5–9). The church confirms the internal call and the approbation of God's people.

A legitimate call manifests itself both internally and externally. It is not enough to have a sense that one is called if no one else confirms it. Neither is it sufficient that a group of individuals or even a church believes a man has the gifts if he senses no call of God on his own life.

Often, during difficult seasons of ministry, I reflect back on the internal call I sensed in those seminary days. But even more so, I look back to the approbation of his people and the formal call I received from a church court (local congregation and presbytery) as confirmation of God's calling on my life. The internal call wasn't a figment of my imagination; others also believed it to be true.

In addition, we discern a call by other necessary elements. I always inquire of young men whether they understand that a pastor principally functions as a servant of God's people. Do they love God, love his Word, and love his people (as I discuss in chap. 8)? These traits require a man of character— a tested and tried character. Poor character clearly evidences that a young man is not called to the pastorate. Being a man of character is fundamental.

Are you called? Begin with the essentials. Do you sense an internal call? Have God's people expressed manifest approval of your gifts and ministry? Do you have the confirmation of the church? If more young men would seek, acknowledge, and confirm all three of these essential elements, it would spare many churches much trouble and spare many pastors much heartache.

3

Candidating

Do your best to present yourself to God as one approved, a worker who has no need to be ashamed, rightly handling the word of truth.

2 Timothy 2:15

Candidating generates an odd dance between a church and a prospective pastor. No one knows for sure who should lead. Concern about stepping on each other's toes dominates the interaction. At times the dance feels intimate and fast-paced, while at other times the parties keep each other at arm's length. Candidating can be encouraging, but it usually proves to be a season of tension, nervousness, and even anxiety—especially for the newly minted pastor.

At the very beginning, commit yourself to prayer. We dare not go where the Lord would not have us. It can be extremely challenging to discern whether God has called you to a particular local church. In the midst of this wrestling, prayer is a necessary means by which the Lord helps us combat our own pride, fears, and tendencies toward being self-serving. As I think back over every new call offered or entertained, the prayer I have persistently uttered is, "Lord, make it clear to me where I am to serve your church. May it not be for my glory, but for your glory. Let it be somewhere I can be of service, bearing fruit in season, among a people who will come to love the truth of your Word; let it be a church where I will love your people well." I have also asked, "Lord, let it be a place where my family will thrive and be blessed by your people."

As you candidate at a church, there will most likely be a pastoral search committee or similar group. It may consist of elders, deacons, laypeople, and even other pastors in the congregation. From the start, resolve within yourself and to the Lord that you will maintain honesty throughout the process. You want the pulpit committee to know who you truly are. Stop yourself from answering questions as you think they would like them answered. Answer truthfully according to your convictions. It is better that both of you discover at the beginning if you are not a good fit for this church rather than finding out months down the road when the heartache and disruption to the church and your personal life could be great.

Some candidates approach a church as if only the church may ask questions—as if the church is the "employer" and the potential "employee" is the passive party. However, pastoral ministry provides a unique context. While the local church pays a pastor's salary, the pastorate surpasses an employer/employee relationship. It is a calling. A pastor needs to discern whether the Lord has called him to serve a particular church. This means you should not be shy in asking questions of the committee regarding the church and its theology, practice, expectations, history, vision, finances, and other areas. A wise course is to ask general questions to see what issues, vision, and passions bubble to the service. But do not be afraid to ask pointed and direct questions as well:

- What is your definition of good preaching?
- What do you expect a pastor's ministry to look like?
- Is the pastor expected to do the majority or all of the counseling, visitations, and teaching?
- What does it mean that the pastor equips the saints for the work of the ministry?
- What ministries of the church does the leadership want to emphasize?
- When were the seasons of struggle in the church, and what caused those struggles?

Listen carefully to their answers and questions. You will learn much by what they say and how they say it. Also listen to what they don't say, which can reveal just as much.

If you are married, be sure to state your own view regarding the role of your wife in the congregation. Ask what they expect of her. Do they want her to coordinate the children's ministry and play the piano? Do they presume she will attend all the functions of the church they expect you to attend? In this conversation, make your own expectations for your wife clear regarding her service in the church. Let them know you consider her first to be your wife; second, to be the mother of your children; and third, to faithfully serve in the congregation as any other member. They are not hiring both of you.

Know how they are going to care for you and your family. Don't be shy in inquiring about the salary and benefits they intend to offer. Refrain from making this the first item you discuss, but it also shouldn't be the last. While we don't enter the ministry for money, "the laborer deserves his wages" (1 Tim. 5:18). Topics may also include vacation time, study leave, retirement, insurance, and housing. Be sure you understand whether "one month's vacation" includes five Sundays or four weeks, whether attendance at conferences counts as study leave, and whether they regularly increase the pastor's salary. In the midst of this conversation, guard your heart and remind yourself that God will ultimately provide for your needs.

Keep in mind that, as a candidate, your great intention is to discern whether God has called you to *this* local church. We serve at the command of the Head and King of the church (Col. 1:18). As such, we are servants. We seek not to be ministered to but to minister to others in the name of our risen Savior. Make the decision to accept a call prayerfully, wisely, and patiently, keeping in mind that you have accepted this call to this particular local church "for life"—until you are unable to physically serve any longer, the Lord brings you home to glory, or he calls you to another field of labor. Therefore, this decision must be made with all seriousness. A particular church must not be treated as a stepping-stone to something else.

PART 2

STARTING OUT STRONG

4

As a Senior or Solo Pastor

Let no one despise you for your youth, but set the believers an example in speech, in conduct, in love, in faith, in purity.

1 Timothy 4:12

The opportunity to serve as a solo or senior pastor is best considered with a sense of caution and humility. A solo or senior pastor faces particular temptations and difficulties most young pastors are not quite ready to endure.

Each of these roles presents its own unique challenges. A senior pastor manages staff, oversees a church, operates a complicated budget, preaches weekly, casts the church's vision, and must garner respect from vocational peers. This role challenges even seasoned men in the ministry. Young pastors need to heavily weigh their ability to handle these responsibilities when deciding whether to take such a call. However, you may be that rare young man. If this is the case, spend your early weeks and months investing in the staff members under your supervision. This initial investment will reap dividends as you seek to minister to them effectively in the future. It will also encourage them to pursue the vision the Lord has given you for the church. These staff members can be either your greatest asset or your greatest liability in the days ahead. They will either work with you or against you. Be a faithful and good pastor to them from the start and earn their trust.

The solo pastorate opportunity usually comes from smaller churches. These churches afford pastors a great place to minister, serve the kingdom, and mature at the same time. The intimacy of the fellowship, the manageable budget, and the limited scope of the ministries can provide sweet blessings as a new pastor gets his feet under him. Every church needs a pastor, and each community needs a faithful shepherd. Do not quickly dismiss the small church that shows interest in you. Always remember that we are servants of the kingdom, not the other way around.

However, you also need to consider that small churches often come with their own difficulties. Tenuous circumstances are quite normal for these fellowships. Limited resources, a lack of energy, an older demographic, and an inflexible attitude of "we have always done it this way" routinely prevail in small churches. These issues can place extra stress on a young pastor and his family. Weigh your own abilities, personality, and gifts as you consider wading into the full responsibilities that come with a solo pastor position.

A senior or solo pastorate requires a measure of spiritual, theological, and emotional maturity. Because age does not define maturity, many young men capably lead in such a capacity. As Paul said to Timothy, "Let no one despise you for your youth, but set the believers an example in speech, in conduct, in love, in faith, in purity" (1 Tim. 4:12). Though young, Timothy evidenced readiness, and Paul did not hesitate in telling him to take the charge.

How do you know whether you are ready? Seek the Lord in prayer and supplication. Do you have sufficient maturity for this particular calling? Ask the Lord to guard you against both prideful ignorance and sinful self-loathing as you examine yourself. Analyze your maturity in Christ. Are you the type of man older saints willingly look to and respect? Do you cast vision and lead in a way that people willingly follow? Can you manage the pressures of weekly preaching, counseling, leading, and shepherding? Will your wife and family ably handle the stress that accompanies your position? Do older pastors who know you well agree that this is a right position for you? If you can answer yes to all of these questions, then prayerfully consider taking that call.

Serve the church effectively, lead humbly, preach the truth, and shepherd that flock. "Let no one despise you for your youth . . . set the believers a good example" (1 Tim. 4:12) by the grace of God.

5

As an Assistant Pastor

Get Mark and bring him with you, for he is very useful
to me for ministry.

2 Timothy 4:11

Most men graduating from seminary desire an assistant pastorate. They realize they would benefit from a few years of ministry before occupying a senior or solo pastorate yet have no inclination toward children's or youth ministry. This makes assistant pastor positions difficult to find and competitive to secure.

Most assistant pastors occupy a designated role within the church. They oversee education, outreach, missions, small groups, congregational care, singles, or fellowship. This can be a wonderful way to begin vocational ministry. It affords the opportunity for a young pastor to grow in confidence, experience, and knowledge without bearing the responsibilities that come with the senior pastorate.

I have served as an assistant pastor in three churches. Based on my experiences, I would encourage you to consider a few things before taking any assistant pastor position. Most importantly, do not take a position unless you respect and like the senior pastor under whom you will serve. I have enjoyed the privilege of laboring as the assistant pastor to three senior pastors—all men I have respected and liked. If that had not been the case, it would have been difficult to continue in the position. Such a situation is unsustainable because a senior pastor sets the vision; his decisions will impact your ministry. You will need to implement his ideas, and you will sit under his preaching. You don't have to like everything about him or agree with every decision he makes, but you must respect him. If you can't in the beginning, don't take the position. If your respect for him disappears in the course of your ministry under him, quietly resign.

A good assistant pastor serves as both a strong leader and follower. Both roles play a crucial part in his ministry. If he is not a strong leader, then few will look to him as a pastor. In such a case, he will be of little help to the senior pastor because a senior pastor will find it difficult to entrust the assistant pastor with tasks, ministries, and his vision for the church. The senior pastor needs confirmed confidence that if he hands something off to the assistant pastor it will be accomplished. He doesn't want to keep checking on him, motivating him, or instructing him. Therefore, a good assistant pastor also needs to be a strong follower. He can be trusted and relied on; he is unfaltering in his outward support of the senior pastor.

This means that an assistant pastor must especially be on guard against offering public criticism about his senior pastor. Parishioners seem to instinctively tune in when harmful words are spoken. If you are dropping hints, they will pick up on them quickly. If you are willing to listen, some may even whisper in your ear that you would make a better senior pastor.

Don't! Stop those conversations before they begin. Support your senior pastor. This is your duty as an assistant pastor in the local church. Yes, you have a responsibility to pastor the people under your care, to fulfill your job description, and to oversee your appointed ministry area, but all of that should be accomplished as you seek to support your senior pastor. This is essential to your call. Not supporting him harms the church more than most young assistant pastors realize. It can disrupt the church's unity and peace in monstrous ways. I am not overstating the importance of this point when I say that you can either be the greatest asset in the local church or its greatest liability.

In that regard, let me encourage you to humbly approach your senior pastor if you consistently find yourself unsettled when he leads and casts vision. If this struggle persists, then move on quietly. It could be a source of pride or arrogance, so make sure to examine yourself for unrepentant sin. However, the Lord often uses this inner angst to move us on to other fields of labor.

Many young assistant pastors hold on too long. Instead of quietly leaving when they feel this inner disquiet, they begin to agitate for change within the local church. They subtly or not-so-subtly begin to work against their senior pastor's vision and reputation in the name of "caring for the church." Don't fall into this trap! Unless an issue of orthodoxy has arisen or the senior pastor is steeped in gross sin or the elders of the church have come to you, don't raise the banner of insurrection. Even if such circumstances present themselves, you should proceed with caution. In most cases, peaceably and graciously moving on is the best course of action.

A good assistant pastorate is a blessing, just as a good assistant pastor is a blessing. Can you lead and follow? Can you support another man? Can you serve behind the scenes? Can you be content not preaching regularly? Can you refrain from gossip and agitating? If so, then maybe the assistant pastorate is for you. If not, then please spare the church that would consider calling you to that role.

||||||||||||

6

As a Youth Pastor

We will not hide them from their children,
     but tell to the coming generation
the glorious deeds of the LORD, and his might,
     and the wonders that he has done.

Psalm 78:4

My first call in the ministry came as a youth pastor. Wonderful memories of those days fill my mind. I am ever thankful for the people in that dear church who gave me the opportunity to teach and disciple their young people. It was one of the great privileges of my life.

However, when first applying for pastoral positions, I didn't sense a particular call to youth ministry. In fact, I tried to avoid it. Thankfully God, in his mercy, had other plans. Like most young pastors, I was convinced that I needed to preach and teach, which is the mind-set of many young men fresh out of seminary. If a solo or senior pastor position is not available, then they are often willing to be an assistant pastor as long as it does not involve youth ministry. Truthfully, some men do not fit well in youth ministry. However, the vast majority of recent seminary graduates would benefit from a few years serving students.

A particular conversation with one of my mentors led me to consider youth ministry. I scheduled a meeting with him in my second year of seminary because it seemed time to begin exercising my gift of teaching in our local church. This pastor politely invited me into his study, where I took up a chair across from his desk. He inquired as to what I wanted to discuss, and I explained I was gifted in teaching and wanted to use that gift for the benefit of our church. He replied, "Great! We will sign you up to start teaching the kindergarten Sunday school class." I quickly protested that this was not what I had in mind. I was not called to minister to children. Didn't he realize I had much more to offer? I was seminary trained! He wisely and rightly said, "Jason, let's give you an opportunity with the five-year-olds. If you can convey the truths of the gospel clearly to them, then you can easily do it with adults." Our conversation ended there. My expectations were dashed, but I soon discovered he was right. If you can teach kindergartners or even high school students the truth of the Scriptures in a way that is clear, engaging, and accurate, then you will be much better equipped to teach adults.

Do you have the gifts of teaching and leading? Don't overlook youth ministry. It is a wonderful place to begin your call as a gospel minister. As the youth pastor, you often have the opportunity to mold and shape the ministry in your own way. You will be challenged to think through organization, process, goals, purpose, volunteers, discipleship, and teaching. You will learn how to minister to mothers and fathers as well as their children, for a good youth pastor engages both students and their parents. The youth will present you with the demands of ministering to the wayward, the lukewarm, the zealous, the discouraged, and the scoffer. You will also be faced with the ever-present temptation to lean on gimmicks rather than to base your ministry on teaching the Scriptures. A man who rises to the challenges in youth ministry will make a better solo or senior pastor in the years to come.

Youth ministry will train you for future ministry. However, it is much more than that. Some of the most lasting fruit of your entire ministry will be born in these students. Many of them will look to you as a key influence on their spiritual lives for the duration of their lives. I haven't been a youth pastor for a decade, yet some of my former students still contact me for advice.

Consider accepting the challenge. Youth ministry is not a lesser field of labor. If you can minister well to students, you can minister well nearly anywhere in the church. Let me add one more word of advice: if you do take such a position, be sure to teach them the Word of God. Play the games, go on ski trips, and eat tons of pizza—but above all, feed them the living and active Word of God (Heb. 4:12). You will be surprised by what they can understand and apply. Labor with and for these children. The blessing will be yours.

7

As a Church Planter

And thus I make it my ambition to preach the gospel,
not where Christ has already been named, lest I build
on someone else's foundation.

Romans 15:20

Have you considered church planting? There are few
better ways the kingdom prospers than the planting
of new churches. I would encourage you to think about the
possibility that the Lord is calling you to start a church.

As you seek to discern whether you are called to church
planting, it is helpful to consider what gifts a church planter
should have. Certainly he must possess gifts in preaching,

teaching, leading, shepherding, discipling, and evangelizing. It is equally clear that he must have some ability to initiate and cast vision for a group of people. He must be a self-starter. No doubt we would also agree that a love for the lost and the underchurched should top the list. Undergirding all these gifts are the essential requirements: that he preaches the Word of God, applies that same Word, and maintains a faithful and active prayer life.

However, I have come to recognize additional qualities that are important for a church planter. I am not an expert on anything (except maybe Chicago-style pizza and Diet Coke), so I don't pretend to be an expert on church planting. However, having served for a number of years as a church planter, my understanding of what is necessary for faithful service in that field has become better informed. There are qualities I had not considered before that I would now say are helpful, if not necessary. As much as young men are needed for church planting, if you aren't marked by the following attributes, then you probably shouldn't rush into this field of labor. A man considering church planting should have the following qualities.

Comfortable in conflict. Who likes conflict? Not many of us. Though the average church planter probably doesn't enjoy conflict, he must be able to endure it. Maybe the greatest difference between church planting and serving in a more established church is that the church planter is usually "out front" by himself. The church is not yet established, so there are typically fewer leaders. This ordinarily means that the church planter must carry the burden of conflict alone—and conflict will come. You don't have to be a prophet to make that prediction. Scoffers need a bull's-eye, and the church planter qualifies as the target. Families require mediation, and they will turn to the church planter as their counselor. Those who gossip are in need of warning, and most likely there is no one else in leadership to do it. A church planter must be able to endure the burden and continue to minister in the midst of it.

Knowledgeable of his weaknesses. There are few buffers between a church planter and the congregation. The smallness of the growing body creates a close physical, mental, and spiritual proximity between the church planter and the congregation. As a result, a church planter will see his weaknesses reflected and adopted by the people under his care—often without their awareness. If he doesn't know his weaknesses at the start, he will learn them over time, at which point significant damage or unnecessary pain may have already developed.

A multitasker. A picture emerges in my mind that we can all recognize: a man holding several sticks with a spinning plate atop each one. How does he do it? I don't know, but it's quite a balancing act. Welcome to the world of church planting. A church planter must be able to multitask. Various areas of church life and ministry will call on him each day. He will engage in everything from preaching to counseling to preparing the order of worship to washing nursery toys. On any given day, he will wear a myriad of hats; he fills the role of secretary, pastor, man on call, emergency ride, and nursery recruiter. While the average senior or solo pastor also functions in many different ways, the church planter usually does so to a greater degree.

Persevering in nature. Let's face it: some of us throw in the towel sooner than others. There are those who labored through two-a-day practices during high school football and others who quit. Some lose a game and never play it again, while others lose and resolve to keep trying until they succeed. A persevering personality is indispensible in church planters because the ebb and flow of church planting is quick hitting and frequent. One week a family visits and shows interest. The next week four families announce they are leaving, and your congregation shrinks in half. There will be weeks, months, and perhaps even years when the average church planter wonders what he has gotten into; in those moments perseverance matters a great deal. It can be the difference between a successful and an unsuccessful church plant.

Able to step aside. While a church planter must persevere, it is equally important that he possesses the ability to step aside if needed. He may labor for years in an area that is difficult for the gospel to penetrate, and his initial zeal and energy may have dissipated. He must know when it is time to hand leadership to someone else or even to close the doors of the work. This requires discerning self-awareness and humility.

Humble. I know. All pastors (and all Christians) are supposed to be humble. But in reality, humility is a rare quality. Among church planters, however, it is an essential quality. Pride will kill the efforts of the church plant and a young congregation quicker than anything else.

Loving of all types of people. While this seems like a practice we should all embrace, it can be a challenge. A church plant draws all sorts of people in a way that well-established churches seldom do. As much as we desire it to be otherwise, established churches often have reputations as the upper-middle-class church, the doctrinal church, the black church, the young church, or the homeschool church. A church plant is seldom marked at the beginning, which means that all varieties of people will come through the door; the church planter must minister to all of them.

Few ministries are more rewarding than church planting. To begin a work with a family or two and by God's grace see it grow into a strong, faith-filled, gospel-proclaiming, established church is a humbling and joyous experience. We need more young men willing to brave these waters. Is God calling you to this work?

PART 3

ENCOURAGEMENTS

8

The Secret and Simplicity
of Ministry

I became a minister according to the stewardship from
God that was given to me for you, to make the word of
God fully known.

Colossians 1:25

Pastoral ministry resembles baseball. Both endeavors
are quite simple, yet we can make them overly complex.
While baseball is pretty straightforward, its simplicity can be
obscured by the intricacies of double shifts, balks, intentional
walks, and obstructing the base path. But at its core, baseball
is simply running, catching, hitting, and throwing—nothing

more, nothing less. Every other aspect of the game remains secondary. Ministry, like baseball, is quite simple. It is nothing more than loving Christ, loving his people, and loving the Word. That is it. When the pastor stands behind the pulpit, these three loves shape his message. When he meets with a man in discipleship, these three loves form his counsel. When he visits a member in the hospital, these three loves direct his visit. This love shapes, forms, and directs a faithful pastor's life and ministry.

As pastors, we must love Christ. The aim, purpose, and end of our ministries is God. We seek no accolades, we need no tribute, and we covet no praise. We are singularly focused on giving glory to God in the person of Christ (1 Cor. 10:31). We desire to see him exalted and magnified. Therefore, we preach Christ (1 Cor. 1:23), point others to Christ (1 Cor. 2:2), and comfort others with the truth of Christ. It is his Word we teach (Col. 1:28) and his hope we extend. Our love for Christ directs, forms, and propels our entire ministry.

However, love for Christ is insufficient. We also must love his people (1 John 2:10). At the end of the Gospel of John, after Peter's threefold denial of Christ, Christ extends to him a threefold restoration. He does so by asking Peter, "Do you love me?" When Peter answers, "Yes, Lord; you know that I love you," Jesus says to him in response, "Feed my sheep" (John 21:17). Love for Christ must be accompanied by great love for his people (Matt. 22:37–39). We can wax eloquent about the hypostatic union and the parousia, but without love we are nothing more than "a noisy gong or a clanging cymbal" (1 Cor.

13:1). Love for Christ's people accompanies love for Christ; these two loves cannot be divorced. This love will drive all our decisions, actions, and motivations in ministry. Christ's people will occupy the forefront of our minds. They will dwell in our hearts. The people of God are to be, as the apostle Paul says, those "whom I love and long for, my joy and crown" (Phil. 4:1). As a pastor, love your people and love them well.

As we love Christ and love his people, it is fundamental that we also love his Word. We love God, so we love to hear his voice (Ps. 119:16). In the Scriptures we have his very real, clear, distinct, and holy voice (2 Tim. 3:16). There is no other living Word (Heb. 4:12). Therefore, as we seek to love his people, we bring this Word to bear on their souls for the glory of God. We have no greater gift to offer those under our care, for nothing can minister to them like the Word of God. No self-help talks, spiritual incantations, practical advice, or earthly wisdom sufficiently attends to the maladies of their souls. Motivated by our love for God and our love for his people, we teach and preach and proclaim his Word.

Ministry can become complex, but one of our jobs as a pastor is to make sure that doesn't happen. Amid all the administration, sermon preparation, meetings, counseling, and visiting, don't lose sight of the simplicity of ministry. When love for Christ, his people, and his Word dominates our motivations and actions, everything else falls into place. Keep your ministry simple, focused, and God-glorifying by keeping it centered on this threefold tapestry of love.

9

Your Early Ministry Focus

Do your best to present yourself to God as one approved, a worker who has no need to be ashamed, rightly
handling the word of truth.

2 Timothy 2:15

I graduated from seminary and was looking for a church to
pastor when a church invited me to candidate. They asked
me to preach a couple of times, and a few weeks later inquired
whether I would be their pastor. Unfortunately, the previous
pastor had introduced theological errors into the life of the
church, and it was embroiled in theological heterodoxy. The
congregation and elders were still trying to decide where they

stood on these important issues. To make matters more difficult, this church was at odds with its denomination's teaching.

I wasn't sure what to do. I wanted to pastor a church, and here was a local body of believers that wanted me as their pastor. But it was a church brimming with problems. By God's grace, an older pastor in the faith gave me some helpful advice. As I shared in the introduction to this book (and it bears repeating), he said, "Jason, don't get entangled in controversies early in ministry. Devote your first years to learning the Scriptures above all else." This was sound, good, and godly counsel. I took his advice and told the church I would not become their senior pastor. I made one of the best decisions of my life.

The apostle Paul writes, "All Scripture is breathed out by God and profitable for teaching, for reproof, for correction, and for training in righteousness, that the man of God may be complete, equipped for every good work" (2 Tim. 3:16–17). As pastors we must resolve to study, live, and teach the Scriptures. Our people need us to know, breathe, and abide in the Word of God. They need us to have a daily encounter with the living Christ through his Word, because it is from this Word that we have something to give them. We teach, reprove, correct, train, and equip on this foundation. Apart from knowledge of the Word, we have no competence in the ministry.

One of my seminary professors once told our class, "Above all else, know your English Bibles." As a proud young man, I rolled my eyes. I knew Greek, Hebrew, theology, ethics, and the basics of counseling, and I arrogantly assumed that knowledge of the English Bible was secondary. But this seminary professor was exactly right. Knowledge of the English Bible provides a foundation for everything else. I will not ultimately help a grieving mother by my counseling techniques; she needs the comfort of the Word. I will not ultimately help a skeptic by my apologetic skills; he needs the truth of the Word. I will not ultimately strengthen a congregation by my pulpit presence; they need the authority of the Word. It is the Word of God that we must know. It alone gives life to our people. We have nothing to offer if we are not grounded on, saturated with, and focused on the truth of God's Word.

There are so many things that will demand your attention in those early days of the pastorate, yet nothing is more important than getting to know the Word of God thoroughly, accurately, and confidently. Immerse your soul and mind and heart in this Holy Word. Spend hours reading it. Steal away moments to meditate on it. Engage in the hard work of memorizing it. Read an entire book in one sitting. Memorize an outline for each of the sixty-six books so that you know what they contain. Discover where in the Scriptures you would point the skeptic, the doubter, the inquirer, or the backsliding Christian. Know where you would turn if someone struggled with depression, anxiety, marital conflict, lust, greed, or pride. Be familiar with what the Scriptures say to the person doubting the reign of Christ, the essence of the gospel, the hope of the resurrection, or the nature of the church. Be able to point people to the passages that have formed your convictions on polity and the sacraments, and your understanding of the decrees of God. Your people need to know that you know the Word of God and that you speak with authority because you are rightly handling the Word of Truth (2 Tim. 2:15). And *you* need to know that you know the Word of God so you can minister with confidence.

I do not offer this advice so that the young pastor can be puffed up in pride or win the church Bible trivia contest (though it does feel good to defeat the high schoolers). The essential thing is to be proficiently reliant on the Word of God in all aspects of our ministry. The Word is our foundation (Eph. 2:20). A ministry that is filled with the truth of God's Word is a ministry that is worth having. If you don't know the Word and aren't willing to work at it, then you should find another vocation. Spare the church and spare yourself. You will never regret the time you spend early in the years of your ministry establishing a thorough knowledge of the Word of God. You will draw on it for the rest of your days, even as you continue to grow in your knowledge of and love for it.

10

Strain Your Eyes

Read Often and Widely

A scoffer seeks wisdom in vain,
   but knowledge is easy for a man of
   understanding.

Proverbs 14:6

It is difficult for a pastor to grow if he isn't reading. There is no way to circumvent this vital aspect of the ministry of the Word to which we have been called. This means we study. We study the Word, the theology of the Word, and the application of the Word. We study the history of the church, false religions, culture, people, philosophy, and current issues. A reading pastor makes a better pastor. Our goal is not to become experts on everything. We don't need to know all the latest trends, journal articles, or educational philosophies, but we do need to be students who continually desire to learn. Our goal is to learn more so that we can communicate the truth of God's Word more ably.

Read often and widely. Reading often is a discipline that creates clarity of thought over time. The more we read, the more we are able to discern truth from error. We can draw from a greater knowledge base and understand the implications of arguments. Reading widely also provides better avenues for communicating truth to others.

Schedule reading. Schedule time each week for concerted, uninterrupted, thoughtful reading. It is amazing how much we can read if we schedule even twenty minutes a day.

Read above your ability. Pastors should regularly read above their level to completely understand. Read books and journal articles that challenge your mental capacity and theological acumen; delve into disciplines you haven't explored. As athletes push their bodies, so we are to push our minds.

Read commentaries. As you work in sermon preparation each week, immerse yourself in a host of different commentaries. Read, devour, and compare. Don't be frightened by commentaries from other traditions. Let your theology be challenged and strengthened by reading broadly.

Read theology. Continue to grow in theological knowledge. Subscribe to a theological journal or two. Many pastors find it helpful to work their way through a systematic theology every couple of years or pinpoint a discipline (such as Christology or ecclesiology) and spend months studying it.

Read history and biographies. History and biographies supply some of the most helpful illustrations for preaching as well as encouragement in the midst of ministry. Read church history, your country's history, and world history. Read biographies of missionaries, preachers, explorers, presidents, generals, and monarchs. The trials they faced, the leadership they exercised, and the principles they lived will inform the way you minister and lead within the church. My own ministry has been shaped by reading the biographies of faithful men and women of God. Calvin's commitment to preaching in the face of opposition, Richard Baxter's pastoral care, David Brainerd's pursuit of holiness, Jonathan Edwards's intellectual rigor, William Wilberforce's courage, William Carey's fortitude, and Joni Eareckson Tada's faith have all shaped me as a pastor. I have learned lessons about leadership and life from the lives of men as various as John Adams, Stonewall Jackson, Theodore Roosevelt, Winston Churchill, Harry Truman, Douglas MacArthur, and Louis Zamperini. History and the people of history have much to teach us.

Read fiction. I love history, but it took years for me to see the benefit of reading fiction. It stimulates creativity and stokes the fires of the imagination—something we all need when ministering to others and preaching. Good preachers understand that their sermons need to be not only faithful but also engaging. Observe how good fiction writers grab the reader's attention through the use of words, phrases, illustrations, and character development, and then apply this knowledge to preaching.

Works of fiction also offer helpful insight into the psyche, experience, and feelings of people. These observations will help to inform your own ministry to individuals as you seek to understand their emotions, thoughts, and actions.

Read old books. Yes, read new books and new ideas, but don't forget about the old books. Read books that stand the test of time. They are classics for a reason. Every "new" idea is built on old ideas, so at the very least, these old books will provide a foundation for understanding everything that is "new."

Be selective. You can't read everything. Start a book only if you think it is worth your time and effort. If a book you've started proves to be otherwise, don't feel guilty about not finishing it. In the same light, you don't have to read every word in a book. Some books are better skimmed, while others are best read with pen and paper in hand. You will know pretty quickly when beginning a volume whether it should be skimmed, read, or slowly digested. Follow your instinct and act accordingly. Don't feel like you have to read every new theological bestseller. The most popular books are often those with the shortest shelf life. A good governing principle to follow: read what benefits your soul and your ministry.

Listen to books. Yes, this chapter is titled "Strain Your Eyes," so while this suggestion doesn't exactly fit, I would encourage you to listen to audiobooks. This has become one of my favorite pastimes. I listen to books while driving in the car, especially books that I would struggle to sit down and read. Redeem the time on your way to appointments and while running errands or driving to a conference. You can "read" a lot of books this way (including the Bible on audio).

11

Shepherd Your First Flock

Caring for Your Family

> But if anyone does not provide for his relatives, and
> especially for members of his household, he has denied
> the faith and is worse than an unbeliever.
>
> 1 Timothy 5:8

I have yet to meet a young man who enters the ministry with the intention of neglecting his family. However, some find that the greatest regret at the end of their ministry is how they overlooked caring for their family in the midst of caring for the church. We are not pastoring our church well if we are not pastoring our families well. And we are not providing for our families well if we are not attending to their spiritual needs.

Paul said that "if anyone does not provide for his relatives . . . , he has denied the faith and is worse than an unbeliever" (1 Tim. 5:8). Though Paul is speaking about material provision, his words also apply to the spiritual needs of our families. They are part of the church, and the Lord has entrusted them to us as our first flock. It is a foolish pastor who forsakes shepherding his own family in the name of shepherding the church.

We could generate a long list of the ways a pastor should care and provide for his family while laboring in the ministry. While the list may be endless (and in some ways overwhelming), I will discuss a few of the most important areas.

As you enter the pastorate or a new church, clearly articulate the expectations you have for your wife with regards to serving the church body (I mentioned this in chap. 3, but it is worth repeating). Make these expectations plain not only to the elders of the church and the congregation but also to your wife. Everyone should know—and your wife first of all—that you expect nothing more from her in the service of the church than you would expect from any other woman in the congregation. In relation to your ministry, she is first and foremost your wife; second, she is the mother of your children (for couples with children); and third, she is expected to serve like any other member of the church—not less but also not more. She may serve more than the average layperson, but that is not your expectation and should not be the church's expectation either. She needs to hear this refrain often from you. Your consistent voice will help to drown out the voices she hears to the contrary (whether internal or external). Affirm your conviction and encourage her frequently.

Recognizing that your wife is a member of the church should also lead you to be careful in the details you share with her about confidential and sensitive matters in the local church. Some pastors make the mistake of telling their wives too little about their day, the church, and their ministry, which leads their wives to feel disconnected. However, in our day it is more common for pastors to tell their wives too much. Because we love them and want them to know where our struggles lie, it is an easy error to make. Our wives serve as our confidants, yet it benefits our wives to *not* know some things about church members or situations.

Pastors would do well to consider the words of Proverbs 10:19:

> When words are many, transgression is not lacking,
> but whoever restrains his lips is prudent.

Keep these two rules in mind: if it could disrupt her worship, then don't share it; if it could lead her to struggle with envy, anger, or hatred toward an individual or a group of people within the church, then keep it to yourself. Your wife is a worshiper in the church and a member of the body. This should always shape your communication with her.

As we think about pastoring our families well, we also want to be intentional about being home in the evenings. A family that is never home together is a family that is in jeopardy.

When I entered the ministry, I committed to my wife that I would not be absent from home more than three nights a week. While some weeks I'm not able to keep this promise (a rare exception to the rule), this commitment has worked well in our home because it safeguards our time together. Maybe this is not the rule for you, but find something that works. Be home. Lead family worship, play with your kids, spend time with your wife, cook dinner, and tuck your kids into bed. It is impossible to shepherd well if you are seldom with the sheep.

A faithful shepherd is also cognizant of the needs of his sheep. Be wise to your own family's needs. Our wives are wonderfully different, and our families will go through various seasons of life. The pastor across town may read a new book every evening because his wife needs less conversational time. Your wife may need more time to converse; if so, put the books down. The pastor across town may travel for days at a time, but your family is burdened when you are absent even one day. If this is the case, the conferences and speaking requests will have to wait until your family transitions into the next season of life. Know your family; keep your family. Jesus is the Good Shepherd who knows his own, and his own know him (John 10:14). Likewise, we must know our sheep.

As you care for your family, use the blessings you have. Too many pastors forsake one of the great blessings of pastoring when it comes to caring for our families: flexibility. Long hours, short weekends, and evening meetings pervade pastoral life. However, a pastor can adjust his schedule in a way that the banker, customer service manager, or retail worker can't. Be flexible regarding the needs of the church and your family. Consider taking a lunch hour to visit your children at school. Reschedule your morning to assist your wife during a stressful week, or arrive late to your study if your child needs to go to the doctor. Count your blessings and use them.

On the other end of the spectrum, do not try to overprotect your family. They will experience both the joy and the suffering of ministry alongside you. That is part of their calling. You can't safeguard them from every conflict, rude comment, harsh word, or critical opinion. Though we may desire to protect our families in every situation, in wisdom we know that suffering can be for their good as much as it is for ours: "For this is a gracious thing, when, mindful of God, one endures sorrows while suffering unjustly" (1 Pet. 2:19).

Pastors who pastor their family well usually pastor the church well. The two go hand in hand. Care for your smaller flock, and the larger flock will reap the benefits.

12

Know Your History

Learn about the Church You Are Serving

Then Samuel took a stone and set it up between Mizpah and Shen and called its name Ebenezer; for he said, "Till now the LORD has helped us."

1 Samuel 7:12

As I have learned from experience, you can benefit greatly from studying your church context. Learn the history of the church and the people you are called to serve. I embark on this task with each new church I am called to pastor. During the first few months I meet with older members of the congregation; I treat them to lunch, and they treat me to stories of the Lord's work over the years.

Ask about the former pastors. Even the short-tenured ones left an impact on the church. Inquire about their strengths and weaknesses, the vision they implemented, which families were close to them, and why they left. You will learn a great deal about the church from these inquiries. Be careful to hear what is said, but also listen for what is left unsaid. If those you speak with never talk about people coming to saving faith in the church, then that may not have been an emphasis of the previous pastors. A pastor left out of an oral history may have been a source of incredible pain. Listen with a discerning and pastoral ear.

Determine to the best of your ability (what I term) the "holy cows" of the church. Every church has things that people just don't want to change. These may include the structure of the service, the choir, the bell on the top of the church, the prayer service in the middle of the week, or the color of the paint in the sanctuary. Make no mistake; every church has their "holy cows." Discover what they are and explore why they are important to this congregation.

Also seek to understand the different seasons of the church. Many will define these by the various pastors the church employed over the years. Don't let that cloud your understanding. Rather, seek to know when the church experienced growth, contraction, turmoil, unity, and fruitfulness. Attempt to separate the chaff from the substance of the conversation. Why does this individual think the church was healthy at a particular time and not at another? If the church changed properties or denominations over the years, seek to understand the impact and history involved in each of these decisions.

Find out what conflicts the church has endured. Some individuals in the congregation may reluctantly relay these details while others may include them as the first thing they desire to tell you. Regardless, explore when the conflicts occurred and their source. Many of the major conflicts may have circled around one issue or a handful of individuals. You will want to know this history so that you don't stir up these conflicts afresh. It will also equip you to ably minister to those who may be a constant source of tension in the congregation. It is possible that past major conflicts weren't handled well by the leadership of the church, and a great deal of latent pain may still exist in the congregation. In the days ahead, this will be critical knowledge as some in the congregation respond with less enthusiasm or even opposition to you or the things you implement.

Investigate the history of the budgeting process, the women's ministry, discipline cases, the implementation of different worship styles, conflicts between families, relationships with area churches, family histories, and anything else that might be pertinent to caring for and shepherding these people. Being a good historian of the church not only preserves the past, but it can also be one of the greatest means for a fruitful ministry in the future. You can avoid errors, hurt feelings, and resentment by taking time to know the history of your local congregation. The church will appreciate that you took the time to learn their history, and you will appreciate how this knowledge informs and aids your ministry among them.

13

Personal Holiness Matters

Keep a close watch on yourself and on the teaching.
Persist in this, for by so doing you will save both yourself
and your hearers.

1 Timothy 4:16

Robert Murray M'Cheyne, the famous nineteenth-century Scottish Presbyterian pastor, once remarked, "The greatest need of my people is my own holiness."[1] At first glance it may seem like M'Cheyne is undermining the gospel with such a statement, but one only has to read a few of his sermons to see the high view he had of Christ and the gospel. M'Cheyne is emphasizing what the apostle Paul shares when he instructs Timothy to keep a close watch on himself (1 Tim. 4:16). Our holiness matters. It is important not only in our salvation but also in the salvation of the people the Lord has placed under our care (1 Tim. 4:16).

A pastor who continually seeks after Christ and grows in holiness pursues the most important thing for his own soul and also for those under his care. They need a pastor who loves and is growing in the Lord to lead them to love and grow. We cannot lead where we have not tread. We cannot give what we do not have. We cannot teach what we do not know. We cannot set an example when we are not passionately seeking the Lord ourselves. Where our affections have grown cold, the church will suffer. When our confidence in the Lord is low, the church will feel the effect. The church requires, by God's design, pastors who are holiness-seeking, faith-building, gospel-preaching, love-motivated, grace-imbibed, affection-stirred leaders of God's people. Men who have a solid grip of the Great Shepherd's belt (1 Cor. 6:19–20; Phil. 3:8–11), know his grace, and live in his truth are the men who we need in our pulpits. This precept cannot be overemphasized and must not be minimized.

As I write this chapter and reflect on this truth, I remember many events I have witnessed over the past two years. I have watched the lives of three Christian pastors destroyed for lack of watching over their own souls (1 Tim. 4:16). Each of them I loved, respected, and counted as a friend. All of them had loving wives and children. Yet, their lusts consumed them. For each of these men, it started small—a look at a website or the brush of someone's hand. Today, all three of these pastors are out of the ministry. One sits in prison, and two of them are separated from their children and wife. Each of them lost his home, his friends, his church, his ministry, and his reputation. Sin is deadly (Rom. 6:23); it can destroy everything in our lives. As pastors, our sin has the ability to harm not only ourselves, our families, and our friends but also the myriad of people under our care. And sin can be incredibly subtle. While we can hide it for a season, over time it will drain energy, effectiveness, and fruit from the lives of the people we serve. If not checked, it can be a tool in our adversary's hands for the hindering and destruction of the spiritual lives of countless others.

Keep a close watch on yourself by maintaining daily quiet times, family worship, and heart-engaged corporate worship. Be men who not only preach the necessity of prayer and daily reading of the Scriptures but who also practice it. A daily quiet time (Matt. 6:6) is essential, and practicing family worship at home is equally necessary for our spiritual lives. By all means, don't forget to worship personally as you gather corporately with God's people each week. Each of these realms of worship provides the opportunity to continue examining your own heart to see where sin might have taken hold. Once a sin is discovered, seek to mortify it by the grace of God. Let us pursue holiness with committed devotion. Never preach a sermon, teach a Sunday school class, or provide a meditation without being affected by the text of Scripture yourself. All of our preparation for public teaching and preaching in the ministry should be aimed at our own hearts first.

Our calling is a holy calling. If holiness does not mark us, then we should not be surprised when it does not mark our churches. There are few things more important in the life of the church than the holiness of its pastors. Remind yourself of this daily as you seek the Lord and care for his people.

14

No One Is Looking over Your Shoulder

Use Your Time Well

Well done, good and faithful servant. You have been faithful over a little; I will set you over much. Enter into the joy of your master.

Matthew 25:21

No bell will ring, no clock will sound, no time sheet will be checked. We schedule our own days. For most pastors, no one will formally supervise, monitor, or look over their shoulder. This means a pastor must manage his own time well for the glory of God and the good of the church. The following suggestions can be helpful in this endeavor.

Divide your days. Divide your day into three segments: morning, afternoon, and evening. Determine the number of segments appropriate for you to spend in recreation, at rest, and with your family each week. Allot the remaining segments for study, sermon preparation, visitations, reading, counseling, administration, and other ministry tasks.

Schedule the important things. Some things should appear on your calendar each week, such as time to pray, study, and be at home with your family. These three areas are non-negotiable. Set these times aside first before filling in the rest of your week. Safeguard these segments to the best of your ability.

Determine your best hours. Some pastors are at their freshest in the morning, others in the afternoon, and still others in the evening. Schedule your sermon preparation and study for whatever time is your "prime time"—when your mind is alert, your thoughts are collected, and your body is awake. This is the most important aspect of your labor, so give it your best hours. Arrange your appointments, administration, and meetings at other times.

Be flexible. A pastor who lacks flexibility in his schedule is doomed to frustration, anxiety, and stress—and so is his congregation and family. Your schedule should be full, but not so full that you can't respond to an emergency phone call, a visitor who stops by, a staff member who desires counsel, or an urgent hospital visitation. A good way to gauge whether your schedule is flexible is to ask your congregation, staff, and family members whether they feel like you are approachable or like they are routinely interrupting something more important (I discuss this more in chap. 28).

Expect long hours. Most full-time pastors should expect to work a minimum of fifty hours per week. Most likely, this number will be higher. Our time is valuable, so nights not set aside for family or rest should be used for study, reading, or visitation. We are caring for the souls of God's people; we should expect the work to be demanding.

Be sure to rest. Some pastors struggle to be diligent in work because no one is looking over their shoulder, but others struggle to get enough rest because no one is holding them accountable to take a break. You will burn out, your church will suffer, your body will deteriorate, and your family will disintegrate if you don't adequately rest. Take at least one day off a week—a day during which you refrain from thinking about the church, the next week's agenda, the parishioners in need of a phone call, or the marriage that is struggling. Also, ensure that your salary and benefit package includes vacation time and study leave. Use every vacation day the church affords you. Don't feel guilty! Enjoy them so that you can return refreshed and ready to give your entire body and soul to the church for yet another season.

As John Piper wonderfully reminds us in his helpfully titled book *Brothers, We Are Not Professionals*, we don't punch a clock, put our time in, and go home. We never cease to be pastors, and as pastors we labor for eternal fruit. We possess a unique calling that involves sacrifice, time, our entire person, and our whole life. Give all that you have, while you have it, for the good of his people and his glory. No one looks over your shoulder except the One who matters. In the end you want to hear, "Well done, good and faithful servant" (Matt. 25:21).

15

They Want to Follow

Leadership

Moreover, look for able men from all the people, men who fear God, who are trustworthy and hate a bribe, and place such men over the people as chiefs of thousands, of hundreds, of fifties, and of tens.

Exodus 18:21

Few things are worse than a leader who doesn't lead. It frustrates the vision of the ministry, the people of the church, and the leadership itself. Every pastor is a leader, but each pastor's leadership will look different according to each man's gifting. Some charge ahead, while others are cautious.

Some are consensus makers; others are forceful. Some are outspoken; others are quiet. The Lord formed each of us uniquely. We shouldn't try to lead in ways contrary to our personalites. Yet, while we are all different, two traits are commonly found among great leaders: confident conviction and articulate persuasion.

The reality is that your church wants you to lead. Sheep desire to follow. They need a shepherd, and the Lord has tasked you. Lead. Confident conviction is where most successful leadership starts. It is nearly impossible to follow someone who is not convinced themselves of the direction they are headed, especially if leading involves instituting change or challenging long-held opinions. Though a leader is marked by confident conviction, this does not imply that he is unwilling to listen to advice or a differing opinion or even to change course. Rather, it means he leads by the convictions the Lord has given him until convinced otherwise. People will readily follow a man with confident conviction.

Of equal necessity is articulate persuasion. Confident conviction will take a vision nowhere without the ability to articulate that vision in a way that persuades the listener. As the old proverb says, "How do you know if you are a leader? Look behind you to see if anyone is following." Very few will follow if they don't understand where they are being led. A leader must articulate his vision in a manner that persuades others. This doesn't mean a pastor has to be dynamic or even the most polished speaker. Apparently, neither Moses (Exod. 4:10) nor the apostle Paul (2 Cor. 11:6) spoke eloquently. In fact, sometimes charisma works against good biblical leadership. Those who have been granted such gifts are often tempted to trust in self rather than the Lord. A good leader in the pastorate articulates his vision for the church with sound biblical reasoning and wise prudence in such a way that God's people are persuaded they are being led to follow Christ to the glory of the Father and the good of their own souls. A faithful pastor does not shrink from saying, "Be imitators of me, as I am of Christ" (1 Cor. 11:1).

Although a pastor seeks to articulately persuade, he also listens to the voices of the sheep under his care and corrects course if necessary. He cannot charge ahead like a warrior in battle; he remembers he is a shepherd. Though he leads with confident conviction and articulate persuasion, his leadership is always marked by care for the sheep. Therefore, he adjusts and alters his way, stopping if he discovers that the direction he is leading is harmful to the sheep under his care.

Pastoring necessitates leading. A good pastor will be a good leader. Take time to learn from those around you. Always seek to grow in leadership, and by all means, exercise it.

16

Lose Control

Equip the Saints

Moses' father-in-law said to him, "What you are doing
is not good. You and the people with you will certainly
wear yourselves out, for the thing is too heavy for you.
You are not able to do it alone."

Exodus 18:17–18

On the heels of chapter 15, this chapter title might strike
you as contradictory to my previous discussion about
leadership. However, it is essential that these two chapters be
understood as complementary and equally necessary. As a
pastor, you have to lose control. Perhaps many of you are ready

to turn the page and skip to the next chapter. You are a natural leader and have sought leadership opportunities your entire life. You know, love, and thrive on control. Hearing someone say "Lose control" seems foolish.

However, losing control is the very thing that we must do in the pastorate. When I say, "Lose control," I don't mean that we should stop leading. As I discussed in the previous chapter, our local church needs leadership; pastors are to lead. However, we don't need to lead everything. Moses learned this lesson from his father-in-law, Jethro (Exod. 18), and it is a lesson that many of us can apply as well. Seeking to control all the decisions, ministries, and programs of the local church will kill you, your church, and your ministry. You will burn out, your church will become immature, and people will stop following. Lose some control and be at peace with it. In truth, the ability to let go points to good leadership.

We are "pastors and teachers" (Eph. 4:11 ESVmg.), and our duty does not include controlling everything. Rather, our duty is to "equip the saints for the work of ministry" (Eph. 4:12). We are failing if our ministry does not equip the saints and provide them with the opportunity to use their gifts. Mature pastoral leaders entrust others with areas of responsibility.

Likewise, we shouldn't personally jump to meet every ministry need. If we fill the void on every occasion, others will never step up. The pastor who complains that his elders never visit anyone in the hospital but is at the bedside of every congregant before their anesthesia has worn off is the cause of his own complaint. He is too controlling, and his church suffers as a result. If you serve a church of a few hundred or more, you probably won't know everyone, and you surely can't personally minister to everyone. Let that be all right. Trust that the Lord will use other dear brothers and sisters in the church. We equip the saints to serve and minister to one another. We don't have to do it all. In fact, we shouldn't do it all.

The wise pastor understands that no matter how much he may "feel" in control, the reality is that he has very little control indeed! We serve a sovereign God and have been given the privilege of serving as undershepherds, but we are not *the* Shepherd. He is. The more clearly we realize this, the more readily it will be expressed in our actions and philosophy of ministry as we seek to empower others and "lose control."

17

Find a Friend

For I have derived much joy and comfort from your love, my brother, because the hearts of the saints have been refreshed through you.

Philemon 7

The pastorate is one of the most people-intensive yet isolating occupations one can have. Everyone in the church and many people in the community know you, and yet, no one *really* knows you. Being a pastor can be a lonely calling. In the midst of this desert, find the oasis of a friend. Entrust yourself to someone who knows you—someone who will give honest feedback and good advice, someone who will encourage your soul and will hold you accountable.

The most natural place to look for this type of friend is in the leadership of the church. A fellow pastor, elder, or deacon may fill this role. He will understand many of the struggles you are experiencing and the situations you are involved in; he can be a great source of encouragement and accountability. However, be careful, slow, and discerning about initiating such a relationship. Finding someone in the church, even in leadership, is not always the best course of action. In fact, I often discourage pastors from doing this very thing. Why? Some of a pastor's most vocal supporters in a church during one season can become his most adamant opposition in the next season. Anything a pastor shares is ready ammunition for detractors. This word of caution is meant to safeguard not only the pastor but also his ministry. A few choice words by someone who has been wrongfully trusted can ruin the future effectiveness of a man's ministry in the local church. This is not to say that no one should be trusted. We don't want to be untrusting or skeptical of everyone, but a pastor needs to be guarded about what he shares and whom he shares it with.

Most pastors find that a confidant is best found outside the local church. Each time I have moved to a new area and pastorate, I have called other local pastors and scheduled lunch meetings with them. You may find a true friend in the ministry over the course of one of these lunches. Many areas also have a pastors' network or fellowship group. Find out what your area may offer and explore possible relationships with other local pastors.

Regardless, find someone who will give a listening ear and good advice. Schedule monthly or biweekly meetings. Minister to them, but also allow them to minister to you. Too often, pastors vigorously minister to everyone else and forget that they are equally in need of ministry. This relationship will require honesty about your relationship with the Lord, your congregation, your elders, and your family. Establish a structure for these conversations that does not allow you to avoid the hard questions.

Ask your friend to probe your soul with pointed inquiries and encourage you with the work they see the Lord doing in you; above all, ask him to pray for you. Knowing someone is regularly, consistently, and fervently praying for you is one of the greatest gifts of friendship in the Lord (Phil. 1:3–5). My friend, you *need* a good praying friend.

In addition to having a friend who knows you, it's good to be able to laugh with someone. Ministry is stressful; it is a blessing to have someone who can take you out of the serious "pastor mentality" for a couple of hours. Find a friend and allow him to be a friend. It will refresh your soul (Philem. 7).

||||||||||||

18

Trust His Means

Rely on the Word, Sacraments, and Prayer

> And they devoted themselves to the apostles' teach-
> ing and the fellowship, to the breaking of bread and
> the prayers.
>
> Acts 2:42

I read a news story recently about a church in Texas that
held a raffle every year. Each Sunday that a person attended
church, he or she received one entry ticket for the raffle. On
Christmas the church was especially generous and gave attendees two raffle tickets. At the end of the year all the raffle tickets
were placed in a large bowl, and the pastor drew out a winning

stub; the winner received a brand-new car. Not suprisingly, the church found that they experienced increased attendance after implementing the raffle. The following year they needed something bigger. People wanted more, so instead of a car they raffled off a house. There are ways to do ministry, and there are ways not to do ministry! You may not be tempted to raffle off a new car, but we all face the temptation to wander from the Lord's appointed means for ministry. We must be exceedingly careful: what we "win" them by, we win them to, and what we win them to, we must keep them by.

The latest gimmicks are just that—gimmicks. Though they may have a wow factor, few new ideas in ministry are helpful. Gimmicks often deny the very means God has appointed for accomplishing his kingdom purposes. The Westminster Shorter Catechism helpfully asks, "What are the outward means whereby Christ communicates to us the benefits of redemption?" The Westminster Assembly answers: "The outward and ordinary means whereby Christ communicates to us the benefits of redemption are, his ordinances, especially the Word, sacraments, and prayer; all of which are made effectual to the elect for salvation." As a pastor, never wander from these ordinary means of grace: the Word, prayer, and the sacraments.

Rely on the Word of God. This is how God chooses to work. The Scriptures alone are "God-breathed" (2 Tim. 3:16 NIV), living and active (Heb. 4:12), the means by which God effectually reveals himself to the lost (Rom. 10:17), and "profitable for teaching, for reproof, for correction, and for training in righteousness" (2 Tim. 3:16). Turning to anything else is foolish.

As pastors, we aspire to establish our ministry on the Word of God. We seek to bring this living Word to bear on the souls of people, and we depend on it for fruitfulness in our ministries. As Terry Johnson has reminded us, we are to preach the Word, teach the Word, pray the Word, sing the Word, and confess the Word.[1] And we are to lead our people to do the same.

A good Word-centered ministry will be saturated with prayer (Col. 1:3–14; Eph. 3:14–21; 1 Thess. 5:17). We know our preaching, teaching, and leading according to the Word will bear no fruit apart from the Spirit attending to the Word. Therefore, we are men who are continually on our knees.

A number of years ago a testimony of a local pastor's faithfulness was shared with me. When this pastor retired after decades of service at the church, the new pastor moved into his office and was unpacking his boxes. As he moved around his new office, he found that the carpet was worn in one spot. He called in the secretary to ask why. She replied, "That is where the former pastor prayed every day for this congregation." That is a faithful pastor. In this way, be a man of prayer. Humbly recognize your complete dependence on the Lord for any and all ministry among his people.

Notice that the Westminster Assembly also emphasizes the sacraments as means of grace that demonstrate before our eyes what we hear from the Word proclaimed (Luke 22:7–23; Acts 2:38, 42). Augustine called them "the visible Word."[2] The sacraments of baptism and the Lord's Table set before our senses the truth of our redemption, the glories of the gospel, and the mercy of our Lord. They are significant, tangible signs of God's grace to us. As more churches use videos and drama in their worship services, it is easier to miss *the* visible means God has already given to his people. Study the glorious truths represented, signified, and sealed in the sacraments. Train your people to value them, love them, and rejoice in them. We neglect the sacraments to our own spiritual harm.

A faithful pastor will build his ministry on the Word, prayer, and the sacraments. He will not deviate to gimmicks or the latest fads. He will stand firmly on the promise that accompanies these ordinary means of grace—they alone are sufficient, because God himself has chosen to use these means to do his kingdom work. Rely and center your ministry on them.

19

Reading Scripture and Prayer

> There was not a word of all that Moses commanded that
> Joshua did not read before all the assembly of Israel,
> and the women, and the little ones, and the sojourners
> who lived among them.
>
> Joshua 8:35

Rightfully, pastors tend to study and think a great deal about their public ministry of preaching and teaching. Counseling and discipleship are also highly valued, and most pastors attempt to grow in knowledge of these disciplines. In addition, we devour books about leadership and even hospital visitation. But very few pastors think about two of the most important public things they do: reading Scripture and praying. Too often we think of these two essential functions of pastoral ministry as addendums to the more important aspects of public ministry, but we do so in error. The church suffers as a result.

Reading Scripture in corporate worship or any other setting is not a casual prelude to preaching or teaching. My friends, we teach as we read the Scriptures! The way we emphasize a word, lower our voice, slow down, or speed up while reading leads the audience to interpret the Word. The careful reading of Scripture publicly should be a discipline that every pastor aspires to grow in.

Take time, effort, and energy to become a good reader of Scripture. Practice reading through the passage you will preach through on Sunday morning. Don't wait until you are on your way to the pulpit to think through how you will read the passage. Your inflection should be natural, your emphasis appropriate, and your tone conducive to the spirit of the text. We have all sat through services in which the pastor reads Scripture in a distracting way. Don't be a distraction. We serve the Word, and our audible reading should help the person in the pew to understand the force, tenor, and message of the passage even before we begin to preach.

Listen to great speakers or narrators of audiobooks to improve your technique. Take time to sit, listen, and think through how the narrator influences the listener by the way he or she reads the text. Make notes and then practice.

Just as the preacher teaches through the reading of Scripture, so he teaches through public prayer. As the congregation hears you pray, they learn to pray. The pastor who enters the pulpit without having thought through his prayers is doing the congregation a great disservice. Preparing for the prayers you offer publicly on Sunday morning doesn't mean you don't trust the Spirit. He is as active and present in your preparation as he is in the service on Sunday.

Therefore, I encourage young pastors to write out their public prayers. These may be pastoral prayers or prayers of adoration, confession of sin, and intercession. While you don't need to take the manuscript of the prayer into the pulpit, you certainly can. The act of writing down words will help you avoid clichés, overused phrases, and unintentional repetitions. In addition, it will help you think through biblical passages so that you can actually pray the Word of God in your prayers.

As a young pastor matures in his ministry, it is probably more helpful to progress toward "studied prayer." With "studied prayer" a pastor doesn't manuscript the words; rather, he studies in preparation for the prayer so that he is not just winging it. He generally knows what he is going to say: he has biblical passages, topics, and a general structure in mind. He then leads the congregation in prayer based on these thoughts but is free to go where his mind and the Spirit lead in the moment. Our people are listening, and they are being taught. Therefore, our prayers can't be shallow, they can't be afterthoughts, and we can't treat them nonchalantly.

Take time to learn to pray and read the Scriptures well in public. This will bless both your church and your own soul.

20

Slow to Speak, Quick to Listen

Listening to Your People

A fool takes no pleasure in understanding,
but only in expressing his opinion.

Proverbs 18:2

A glaring fault in many, if not most, pastors is that they are poor listeners. In fact, I find pastors to be some of the poorest listeners I have been around—and young pastors are sometimes the worst offenders. Please don't misunderstand me; this is not true of all pastors, but it is true of many. And it should grieve us.

In my experience, pastors tend to be poor listeners for several reasons: (1) they are usually assertive individuals who have trouble slowing down; (2) they hear many of the same things multiple times (counseling situations, theological questions, etc.) and feel like they know where the conversation is headed; (3) they are multitaskers who tend to assume they can listen and think about other things simultaneously; and (4) they are used to others listening to them preach. That being said, we have no excuse; pastors should be good at listening. It is difficult to minister to the people of Christ if we don't know them. It is hard to know them unless we lend a listening ear. Let me suggest a few ways to be a better listener.

Sermons are for the pulpit. Leave sermons to the pulpit and enter into dialogue with your people. Dialogue requires talking *and* listening.

Remember that the person before you is the person you are called to minister to. Seize the moment and focus on the person before you instead of thinking about talking to the person on the other side of the room. (I discuss this more in chap. 21.)

Be teachable. We may be called to teach, but that does not mean that we can't be taught. Remember Proverbs 4:5: "Get wisdom; get insight; do not forget, and do not turn away from the words of my mouth."

Show honor to all. First Peter 2:17 says, "Honor everyone." The five-year-old or the mentally disabled person begging for your attention and conversation after the worship service is just as important as the district attorney and his wife who are walking by.

Silence is golden. Silence in conversation is fine. The tension it creates is not a bad thing because it often helps to bring the true issues to the surface. Don't feel like you always need to fill the silent void.

Maintain eye contact. Pastors tend to be multitaskers, letting their eyes meander or thinking they can check email on their smartphones as they listen. Stop!

Ask questions. Avoid jumping to conclusions and giving a stock answer. Ask qualifying question after qualifying question.

Don't always feel the need to lead. Most pastors are leaders and feel they need to lead all the time. In conversation, they are no different; they often dominate. At times, allow others to lead the conversation. You will be surprised at what they may want to talk about.

Don't be "superspiritual." Every conversation does not need to end with a discourse on the atonement. Nor does every conversation need to be a forum for you to demonstrate your Bible knowledge.

Think through questions. On your way to a meeting with someone make a mental list of questions to ask him or her. When you meet, ask the questions and actually listen to the responses.

Care tenderly. Always remember that these are Christ's sheep (John 10). They are his, and we are to lead them with tender loving care. Certainly this includes listening to them.

Most pastors I know love the Lord and love the people under their care (Mark 12:30–31). However, if our people don't sense this love, they might doubt it. If we truly listen to our people, we will find that not only are they blessed but also so are we. Listening to God's people proves to be one of the most enjoyable exercises in life. What stories God has given each person, and what a gift it is to hear of the Lord's work in their lives. What passions each individual has—what sorrows, discouragements, and fears reside in every person we meet. Each of them cries out for a listening ear. In the midst of that listening, the Lord opens new avenues for us to minister and be ministered to for the good of the kingdom and his glory.

21

Ministry before Our Eyes

I want you to know, brothers, that what has happened to
me has really served to advance the gospel, so that it has
become known throughout the whole imperial guard
and to all the rest that my imprisonment is for Christ.

Philippians 1:12–13

How often have you been engaged in conversation with
someone on Sunday morning only to find yourself
thinking about the person you need to talk to on the other side
of the room? When our minds start to wander, our eyes often
follow. Thoughts may race through your mind: *I need to talk
to the man over there. If she leaves before I am able to encourage*

her, an opportunity will be lost. No one is interacting with that visitor. In the meantime, you have lost the moment of ministry the Lord has given in the person before you.

The seminary I attended employed a chaplain. One of my professors told a story about him that has always stuck with me. He recalled a day when he was engaged in conversation with this chaplain and the president of the seminary entered the room. A boisterous and charismatic personality, the president is the sort of person who automatically draws attention when he enters a room. The professor recalled how the president made his way over to them, but the chaplain's eyes never diverted from the professor. The seminary president stood waiting on the edge of their conversation, and only after the chaplain had fully ended the conversation with the professor did he turn to the president. It wasn't an act of rudeness or power that led the chaplain to keep the president waiting; it was an act of love and true humility. The professor recalling this story said, "When the chaplain is with you, it is like you are the most important person in the world." The chaplain focused on the professor as his field of ministry in that moment. The Lord gave him this appointment, and he wasn't going to miss it.

I wonder how often we miss the ministry before us for the ministry "over there." How often do we neglect the opportunity we have now because we think there is something more important on the other side of the room, back at the office, or on our phone? I wonder how often we have injured our brothers and sisters in Christ or our witness to the love of God by treating others as insignificant and not worthy of our attention.

Some of the most important ministry we offer as Christians happens in the unplanned and unforeseen moments. Think back over your own Christian life. If I were to ask, "What is some of the most important advice you have received from others?" most of us would point to rather "insignificant" moments. Perhaps you might think of an occasion when someone offered a short phrase or two, like my professor did about the chaplain; or perhaps you might remember a time when it wasn't so much what the person said, it was just the way he or she listened—in the same way that the chaplain influenced my professor. He simply modeled love and grace in the moment. Don't miss the ministry before you. It is there by God's appointment.

22

You Can't Do Everything

Busyness and the Pastorate

And he said to them, "Come away by yourselves to a desolate place and rest a while." For many were coming and going, and they had no leisure even to eat.

Mark 6:31

You can't do everything in ministry. It's impossible. The expectations of others and the expectations we place on ourselves can be met only by a superhero. My fellow pastors, I hate to tell you this, but you are not a superhero. You are an ordinary person with an extraordinary calling, but you are still ordinary.

Jesus sent out the twelve disciples in Mark 6. They went out two by two and "proclaimed that people should repent" (v. 12); "they cast out many demons and anointed with oil many who were sick and healed them" (v. 13). When the disciples returned from ministering in this way, the Lord Jesus had compassion on them and sought to draw away with them to a desolate place that they might rest for a while (v. 31). He gave them rest because he knew they were tired. Our Lord Jesus knows full well that he calls ordinary men to extraordinary service. You can't do everything all of the time; you can't do everything even part of the time. If you try, you will burn out, and years of ministry will be lost. How do we combat this inclination?

First, a good pastor learns to prioritize. He realizes he cannot meet everyone's expectations, let alone the false expectations he places on himself. Spend the majority of your time in prayer, study, teaching, and preaching. Other activities, though often good, should take a backseat to these priorities. This means a pastor must say no to many things that are asked of him. Every request, demand, email, phone call, and meeting you agree to requires saying no to something else. We have only a certain number of hours in the day. You may disappoint the mother who wanted you to attend her son's baseball game, the young couple who desperately desired you to do their premarital counseling, or the elder who was upset you didn't make it to the hospital. That is OK. You should go to *some* baseball games, do *some* premarital counseling, and make *some* hospital visits, but you must know when and whether you are able. Prioritize your schedule.

Second, take your vacation days. I once stood among a group of pastors who were attempting to outdo one another in conversation by comparing how few vacation days they actually took in the past year, as if this were some badge of honor. Not taking your vacation days isn't a sign of godliness; it is a sign of foolishness. As pastors we can't take long weekends. We work many evenings and long days, and our labor is stressful, which can take a real toll on you and your family. This makes it absolutely necessary for you and your family to regularly get "away by yourselves to a desolate place and rest a while" (Mark 6:31). If Jesus thought this was necessary for the disciples, then maybe it is a good idea for us too! Ask your church to give you three to five weeks of vacation a year. In addition, ask them for an annual week or two of study leave. Then use all of it.

Third, ask your wife and elders to hold you accountable about the use of your time. They should ask whether you have been spending an adequate amount of time in prayer, study, and preparation for preaching. If you haven't, then your scheduling of priorities must change. Allow them to inquire as to how you employ your free time, whether you observe a day of rest, and how you use your vacation time. Give them the right to confront you at any time if they think that you have stumbled into a superhero complex.

We can't do everything. Most congregants will be understanding; they are people too. However, they need their pastor to come to grips with this reality first.

23

If You Pastor, They Will Come

Listening to Complaints

A rebuke goes deeper into a man of understanding
than a hundred blows into a fool.

Proverbs 17:10

Different people will respond in different ways to your ministry. In fact, different people will respond in different ways to the same sermon. Two individuals separately approached me after a sermon I once preached. One told me, "You are legalistic." The other told me, "You are an antinomian." They couldn't both be right. I hope neither was right!

Complaints will come as you minister. People in the congregation will complain about your preaching, leading, decision making, or lack thereof. They may object to how far the house you bought is from the church or to the way you run a meeting. Jonathan Edwards's congregation (eighteenth century) complained that he had two powdered wigs. How dare he! What extravagance! Recently, a pastor told me he was confronted for not wearing his suit coat to the church's evening service. He apologized before preaching for having forgotten it at home, yet people in his congregation still voiced their dissatisfaction with him when the service ended. I once had a man tell me he would never respect me as a pastor because I went on a three-hour car drive with my family on a Sunday afternoon to visit a family member. He felt I was somehow violating the Lord's day. Some complaints are silly, others can be hurtful, but some are helpful.

We don't need to seek complaints because they will come regardless. Many young pastors are shaken by the dissatisfaction that members or leaders of their congregations express. They didn't realize this would be part of ministry. Expect complaints and be prepared for them.

When complaints come, we must be willing to listen. A good pastor will remain teachable. He needs the same admonition, correction, and training in righteousness that every member of the church needs (2 Tim. 3:16). Even if the complaint is inaccurate, there may be motivations behind it that are helpful to know and understand. For example, a woman may approach you after a service and complain that your sermon was too negative and not hopeful enough. That may be accurate, but it might also signal that she struggles with discouragement and yearned for a more encouraging word that morning. When a complaint comes, receive it. Fight the inclination to be defensive, and be willing to pray about the correction offered.

While we must remain humble and willingly listen to the concerns of the people we serve, it is unnecessary to entertain every complaint. Some complaints are ridiculous and can be quickly disregarded. They are not worth the sleepless nights, hours of introspection, or questioning that can follow. The sooner we realize this as a pastor, the better.

When I receive a complaint via email or letter, experience has taught me that such messages are best handled in person. Written forms of communication allow individuals to express a more vehement attitude than they would dare offer in person. The waters tend to calm when the discussion takes place face-to-face. Even more important is the reality that most of us are much more effective in conveying tone and tenor in person than we are in written forms of communication like letters and emails.

Try to develop a thick skin, but cultivate a tender heart. Don't take complaints too personally. Remind yourself that criticism comes with leadership. You are a focal person in the church, and some people feel the need to direct their anger, hang-ups, and dissatisfaction at someone. Because of your visible leadership position, you just happen to be the most viable option. More people will express opinions about what we say, do, or don't do than about anyone else in the church. That is to be expected as part of leadership. Develop a thicker skin so that you can receive the number of complaints that will inevitably come your way. However, even as you attempt to have thicker skin, always maintain a tender heart. Stay humble, stay loving, cherish the people of God, and rejoice that you get to serve them.

24

Silent Suffering

He was oppressed, and he was afflicted,
yet he opened not his mouth;
like a lamb that is led to the slaughter,
and like a sheep that before its shearers is
silent,
so he opened not his mouth.

Isaiah 53:7

The call to suffer reigns as one of the most unique things about the Christian life (Matt. 10:38; John 16:2; Rom. 8:17; Phil. 1:29). If anything about the faith is countercultural, this surely is it! However, it is not only the call to suffer that forges this wholly different ethic; it is also the courage to endure that suffering silently, which is often a mark of good leadership in the church. Don't misunderstand me; there are certainly times when we should not endure suffering silently. We dare not be silent when the gospel is at stake. But our suffering for the sake of Christ usually does not call for us to add our voice to the cacophony.

When persecuted or falsely accused by others, our first inclination is typically to offer a defense. Why is that? In most of these cases, our true concern is not the gospel, or Christ, or even his church—though those may be secondary concerns. Most often, our true motivation is what others will think of us if we don't respond. The ever-present desire to be vindicated galvanizes us.

The rationalizations come fast: "I cannot allow error to triumph over truth"; "My reputation is at stake"; "It will hamper my future ministry or current relationships"; "I know I am to suffer, but that does not mean being a doormat." Despite these rationalizations, it is usually wise to follow the lead of our Lord and suffer silently (Isa. 53:7; 1 Pet. 2:23–24). It is not easy, but often it is the most righteous and holy course we can take. You will suffer in ministry. If God calls the Christian to suffer, how much more so the pastor who represents Christ to his people? As Peter says, in so doing we are following in his footsteps (1 Pet. 2:21–25). Here are a few reminders as we seek to suffer silently unto the glory of God.

We have been given the following opportunities:

- To test our desire for God's glory rather than human approval (Isa. 51:7–8)
- To look to Christ, who suffered silently (Isa. 53:7)
- To truly love our enemies (Matt. 5:44)
- To remind ourselves that the Great Judge knows what is true (Matt. 12:36)
- To learn afresh how dependent we are on Christ (John 15:5)
- To be identified with Christ (John 15:18–21)
- To suffer with him, knowing that as we do, we shall be glorified with him (Rom. 8:17)
- To know more fully the extent of Christ's love toward us (Eph. 3:14–19)
- To complete what is lacking in Christ's afflictions (Col. 1:24)
- To be tested by fire so that the genuineness of our faith will shine to the glory and honor of Christ (1 Pet. 1:7)
- To suffer because it is a gracious thing in the sight of God (1 Pet. 2:20)
- To become more like Christ as we endure suffering (1 Pet. 2:21)
- To share in suffering with Christ (1 Pet. 4:13)
- To suffer because it is a blessing and a sign that the Spirit of glory and of God rests on us (1 Pet. 4:14)
- To be reminded that our current suffering is nothing compared to the glory that awaits (1 Pet. 5:10)

Fear of man must not silence us when we should speak (as when the gospel is at stake), but neither should it lead us to speak when we should not. Suffering for the sake of Christ often means remaining silent in the midst of suffering. It is hard and can be a bitter pill, but as our minds are gripped by these truths, that which is hard and bitter can also be sweet.

25

Thankfulness for the Congregation

I thank my God in all my remembrance of you, always in every prayer of mine for you all making my prayer with joy.

Philippians 1:3–4

Dear pastor, thank God for the congregation you serve. God has gifted us with these people, though some individuals may seem to be more of a gift than others! While some people are more difficult and it is far from easy to consider them a gift, notice Paul's prayer in the first chapter of Philippians. It is not exclusionary. He prays and thanks God in verse 4 for "you all." His thanks are offered for every person. Though we may be quick to say, "Of course this church supported Paul while he was imprisoned. This congregation treated him with care and respect. They were loyal to him," Paul's church was not historically unique. The modern era doesn't maintain the sole contract on problem people and problems in the church. Some of these people caused Paul real anguish. In Philippians 4, we find that Euodia and Syntyche refused to agree with each other. They fought and appeared to lead women in the church to take sides, yet Paul prayed a prayer of thanksgiving for all of them—including Euodia and Syntyche. Paul knew the problems in the church and who caused them. However, he was equally aware they were *all* a blessing from God.

You may think, *But there was only one conflict in the Philippian church*. I seriously doubt that was the case, but when we turn to Paul's First Letter to the Corinthians we find division, a party mentality, the questioning of Paul's authority, sexual immorality, lawsuits against other believers, raging debate about marriage and food sacrificed to idols, idolatry, abuse of the Lord's Table, and conflict over spiritual gifts. This church defines dysfunctional! Yet Paul opens the letter by saying, "I give thanks to my God always for you" (1 Cor. 1:4).

How could he do such a thing? Because he knew that we are gifts to one another. The members of your church are a gift no matter how messy and difficult the church is. As we think about, pray for, and minister to our congregations, do we appreciate the blessing each person is within it? Do we thank God for all of them? Paul writes to the church in Philippi, "Therefore, my brothers, who I love and long for, my joy and crown . . ." (Phil. 4:1). The church would be well served if this was the heart cry of every pastor of every local church. Thank God for the people you serve by his appointment and his grace. They are a gift—a gift to you.

26

Dual Purposes

The beginning of wisdom is this: Get wisdom,
and whatever you get, get insight.

Proverbs 4:7

The pastorate is busy, so adapt the things you engage in to serve more than one purpose. This is the better part of wisdom. You won't have time to create every lesson, teaching opportunity, or blog post from scratch. A well-organized and thoughtful pastor will repurpose material in multiple ways.

For example, sermons easily turn into blog posts and columns for the local newspaper. The entirety of your study on a passage cannot be relayed in one Sunday sermon, so turn extra material into articles for the monthly church newsletter. Even articles and books can flow from your study for preaching and teaching. When studying for a sermon, keep detailed notes on the passage and topic. File away all the exegesis, commentary reading, illustrations, and contextual considerations. The next time you return to that passage for a Sunday school class or other occasion, those notes will simplify your task.

As you read, select books that not only feed your soul but will also inform upcoming teaching, preaching, and writing. Again, take detailed notes and file them away. Highlight passages in books with different colors that signify their different applicable uses: yellow for a sermon illustration, orange for teaching, and green for a writing project.

When called to preach at another local church, conference, retreat, or even wedding, recycle a sermon. Of course, you will want to tweak it and make certain that your heart and soul are still affected by it before preaching it again, but a sermon preached a second time is not a sign of unfaithfulness. If it was good enough to preach once, it is good enough to preach twice.

Reading and sermon study also provide ready answers for counseling. Memorize passages you are preaching from that could be helpful in a counseling situation. Keep notes on helpful illustrations that may connect with a counselee.

A little resourcefulness and thoughtfulness about how to use things for dual purposes can increase your productivity and lessen your stress for the good of the kingdom. It can make the difference between an overtaxed and a manageable ministry.

||||||||||||

27

Administration to the Glory of God

It is not right that we should give up preaching the word of God to serve tables.

Acts 6:2

Who knew that administration pervades church ministry? Not me. I was shocked in my first pastorate to discover so much of my time could consist of pushing papers, answering emails, receiving phone calls, recruiting volunteers, filing paperwork, organizing meetings, setting agendas, editing minutes, and figuring out staff health insurance. I am tired just thinking about it! The idyllic view of spending half the day in my study reading the Bible and the other half visiting people in their homes quickly vanished. In some ways, administrative duties are necessary; in other ways, they are a travesty.

Administration is a "necessary evil" of ministry. A pastor who neglects administration does so at great risk. However, it must be kept in balance. I knew a pastor who spent his first four years at a church working with the elders to write a policy for every conceivable issue in the church. After four years, the elders had debated, agreed to, and implemented a six-inch binder filled with policies. In the middle of that fourth year, the church fired the pastor. The binder now sits on a shelf and collects dust. Though the church had a policy for every conceivable situation, the church itself was neglected. Administration took over that pastor's ministry.

Administration creep occurs subtly and easily. We can go through a day of ministry answering emails, returning phone calls, and organizing policies with very little personal ministry taking place. A week can pass in this way, and all of a sudden we realize that we have devoted more time to administration than to studying the Word of God, praying, and meeting with people. Our pervasive administrative duties have encroached on our time and taken over.

Remember that administration in the church serves the ministry of the church and not the other way around. A paper cup is useful only so far as it is filled with water. While it simplifies the act of bringing water to parched lips, it is never an end in itself. The same can be said of administration. It is helpful only insofar as it brings the living water of Christ to the souls of parched people. Don't do administration for the sake of administration. Only engage in the necessary—nothing more. Administration is a monster with an unceasing appetite that will consume all your time if you allow it.

Try to pass off as much administration as you can to lay-people, the church secretary, or other support staff. "It is not right that we should give up preaching the word of God to serve tables" (Acts 6:2). We want to primarily "devote ourselves to prayer and to the ministry of the word" (Acts 6:4). That is our calling. We should undertake administration only when it serves that end. This is executing administration to the glory of God.

28

Leave Your Door Open

I became a minister [of Christ's body, the church] according to the stewardship from God that was given to me for you.

Colossians 1:25

There are no interruptions in ministry, only God-ordained providential opportunities. The sooner a pastor realizes this truth, the better he will serve the people of God.

We believe in a sovereign Lord and that God has called us to ministry for the sake of others. Therefore, no person and no event is an interruption in our ministries. Paul declares in Colossians 1:25 (as well as in passages like Rom. 11:13–16;

1 Cor. 9:16–23; and Gal. 1:16) that God called him as a minister for the sake of others; the same is true of us. This means that the pastor must primarily see himself as a servant of the church. He is not its lord, its CEO, its president, or its head. Rather, he serves as the chief servant of his local congregation. Therefore, when others come calling, he is alert and ready to serve. It is no accident that they have walked through his door.

This mind-set helps to relieve many difficulties in the pastorate. A pastor so resolved is a man who leaves his door open. I am not arguing that his study door must always be ajar but rather that this mind-set will persist as his dominant attitude toward others. We want everyone to sense that they are never a bother or burden to us. They may stop by with an immediate concern, send an email seeking counsel, or call when they are in need of prayer.

Having said this, we don't want to neglect setting priorities (as discussed in chap. 22). We must attend to our necessary work of study, preparation, and prayer. As our main priority, this work cannot be hampered. However, we should be available, willing, and flexible when others "impose" on us and "disrupt" our schedule; we serve others at the call and behest of the Lord of the church.

If you aren't working on a sermon or engaged in prayer and can handle the noise outside your study, leave the door open. Even if your door remains closed and someone knocks on the door, you should lift your head from your book or back away from the computer, give eye contact, and show your staff member, congregant, or visitor that they are welcome. They are not a bother, and they have your full attention; they matter because they are his sheep.

Guard yourself against being a pastor who always seems too busy for others. Such a pastor views his study as a place of escape, and everyone knows he can't be disturbed. He expresses frustration when someone calls, stops by, or even sends an email. Over time the people of the church, fellow staff members, and elders sense they can't bother him, which prevents many wonderful opportunities for ministry to develop and occur.

Our schedules each week can be carefully planned and full, but they should never be uncompromising. Build in flextime to help prevent frustration when someone knocks on your door or the phone rings. The pastor who is too busy in his study with his daily list of tasks will find that the lord of his ministry is not who it should be. As the days, months, and even years pass, many boxes will be checked off, but many souls will remain unaffected because of opportunities lost.

29

Weddings and Funerals

This mystery is profound, and I am saying that it refers
to Christ and the church.

Ephesians 5:32

Officiating weddings and funerals is one of the greatest privileges of gospel ministry. Families gather from all over the country and sometimes even the world for these events. While weddings are times filled with excitement, promise, and hope, funerals tend to be occasions filled with sorrow, disappointments, and fears. Emotions at each of these gatherings are palpable, and people are open to gospel ministry in unique ways. Some of the most eternally significant ministry you engage in will occur with people at these events.

Many people will never darken the door of a church except to attend a marriage or funeral. Some attendees will be foreign to the stories from Scripture, the verbiage of Christianity, and the doctrine of the church. Therefore, at every wedding and funeral preach a sermon that is solidly biblical and gospel saturated. It should be clear, concise, and appropriate for the moment. You are preaching to a different audience at these services, and your sermon should reflect it. If one attentively reads the sermons of Jonathan Edwards, it is interesting to observe that he preached considerably more complex sermons in the church at Northampton than he did later in life among the Mohican Indians as a missionary. He adapted to his audience, and so must we.

At wedding and funeral ceremonies, clearly demonstrate that you are in charge. You are leading a worship service, and it should be conducted as such. As the pastor, set guidelines for what is appropriate and what isn't within the services. I worked with a pastor who recalled a funeral he conducted at which a nephew of the deceased desired to sing a song he had written. The pastor gave permission without hearing the lyrics or the tune. It was a huge mistake! Hearing the aunt's name sung to the tune of Rodgers and Hammerstein's "Oklahoma" was something no one was prepared for.

Maintain leadership over these services, but don't be inflexible. A bride and groom should offer a great deal of input, just as a grieving family should influence the order of service for a lost loved one. However, the final decision is yours as a pastor. Sometimes this means you need to say no to a certain song, eulogy, or processional.

Be sensitive to the dynamics within a family as you conduct a wedding or funeral. Learn as much as you can about the family before the actual wedding rehearsal or visitation for a funeral takes place. This knowledge allows you to navigate sensitive waters and avoid potential conflicts. If conflict is obvious, you may need to give directions on who sits where and when certain individuals can attend or not attend a rehearsal. Quickly find out who "reigns" as the matriarch or patriarch of the family. Befriend them and use their authority to settle issues beyond your control that could potentially ruin such an event.

Consider weddings and funerals an opportunity not only for you to minister to others but also for your local church members to serve. Equip your church with this mind-set. A hospitality team for funerals provides an unexpected blessing; furnishing a meal after the funeral yields a wonderful encouragement. Likewise, assisting the bride with a church-appointed wedding coordinator renders a smoother wedding day. Seize the opportunity to demonstrate the grace of the Lord Jesus in ways that those in the world seldom see.

As the years pass, you will mature as an effective minister in both of these services. Never take them for granted. It is a privilege to serve a family, the church, and God in such a momentous way.

30

Hospital Visitations

Is anyone among you sick? Let him call for the elders
of the church, and let them pray over him, anointing
him with oil in the name of the Lord.

James 5:14

Hospitals afford fertile ground for gospel ministry. Before my ordination I served as a pastoral intern at a large church in Dallas, Texas. Each week a pastor on the church staff visited all the members of the church and their relatives admitted to area hospitals. This routinely consisted of calling on fifteen or more people scattered across various hospitals in

132

the region. Many weeks the pastors were unable to make the visits, so the church secretary would call forth us lowly interns.

There were two of us serving as interns, so we would divide up the list before setting out to complete our visits. For a period of about four weeks, we made all of the hospital visitations. Each week I received the name of a woman and the hospital where she was located. She was the only person from our church in that hospital, and it happened to be on the other side of town. It took me forty-five minutes of driving just to reach this particular hospital. For three weeks, I picked up my Bible, made the visits on my list, and then journeyed across town to call on her. Each time I knocked on her hospital room door and announced who I was, and on each occasion she yelled from her bed that she didn't want any visitors that day.

On the fourth week I received her name again. I was (understandably) hesitant to make the trip as I had done the previous three weeks. It seemed like a waste of time. Aggravated by this thought, I convinced myself not to visit her. I made my other hospital stops and began driving back to the church. The closer I came to the church, the more my conscience was pained. The Lord convicted me of my self-centeredness and lack of love. I reluctantly turned the car around and headed across town. When I arrived, I knocked on her hospital room door as I had on the previous three occasions, expecting to be summarily dismissed. However, this time she invited me in. When I entered the room and peered at the bed, I saw a young woman propped up on pillows. She appeared to be in her mid-twenties. I immediately noticed she had no arms; I took another look and saw she also had no legs. Her entire person consisted of a torso and head. She then proceeded to ask for *my forgiveness* for not feeling well enough to invite me in on the three previous occasions. She relayed the awful pain that she has to endure each day. On the previous days I had attempted to visit her, she was experiencing excruciating pain that prevented her from conversing with anyone. Over the course of our conversation, she informed me that this stretch in the hospital had lasted 120 days. During the half hour I visited with her, she spoke about the Lord and the things of God. As I walked away, a jarring thought entered my mind: *She ministered to me.* I had grumbled about my duty to visit and bless her and walked away as the one blessed. On that day, the Lord convicted me of the great privilege pastors have of visiting the sick and dying in the hospital. I vowed never again to complain about this duty.

As you make hospital visits, have Scriptures in mind that you might read and pray through at the bedside of the patient, but also be willing to allow the Spirit to lead in the moment. When visiting, ask how the patient is doing, inquire as to how you can pray for her, read a short portion of the Bible, and pray. Even those who are most antagonistic to the gospel are willing to listen to the Scriptures when they are lying on their deathbed. Don't spend all your time talking about the weather, their family members, or even their illness. All these things serve as good conversation pieces, but they should not replace or marginalize your reading of the Scriptures and prayer.

Keep your visits short. Most patients are weary from the constant parade of nurses, doctors, family members, and technicians entering their room. We don't want to add to their burden. Always look for family members and friends of the patient in the waiting room and hallway. Some of the best ministry opportunities in the hospital will occur with those who are grieving, anxious, or discouraged because their loved one is sick or dying. It the midst of your visits, don't neglect the doctors and nurses. You will see many of them on a regular basis. Establish relationships by introducing yourself, jot down their names, and refer to them by name the next time you see them.

Amid all the various opportunities you will enjoy over the course of your ministry, hospital visits will play a central and meaningful role. These places of suffering, affliction, and mercy make fertile soil for the bearing of much fruit.

31

Leading Meetings

And all the assembly fell silent, and they listened to
Barnabas and Paul as they related what signs and wonders God had done through them among the Gentiles.
After they finished speaking, James replied, "Brothers,
listen to me."

Acts 15:12–13

Few men enter the pastorate with any concept of how
many meetings they will attend. The pastorate is filled
with meetings, and you will often lead them. Small group, one-
on-one, and staff meetings occur every week. While they are
important to prepare for, these kinds of meetings are generally

simple to lead. Therefore, this chapter addresses the larger meetings that take place with elders, deacons, the congregation, and committees. As you think about leading large meetings, keep the following guidelines in mind.

Set an agenda. An agenda is always helpful. It allows the participants in the meeting to know the plan for the meeting, which will hopefully inform discussion, halt unnecessary tangents, and provide overall structure. In the agenda, allot time for each item. Be realistic in that allotment but also conservative in the estimated time given. This helps to move the meeting along at a quicker pace. In my first pastorate, many elder meetings began at seven o'clock in the evening and didn't finish until midnight. On most occasions this was unnecessary. They ran late because the meetings weren't led well. It is unfair for the layman, who has to rise early in the morning and be at the factory or office by six o'clock, to be kept that late by church business when a well-ordered agenda could have prevented it. Respect the men and women you labor with by setting an agenda and sticking to it.

Place important issues early in the agenda. It is often helpful for the first item on the agenda (after prayer and Bible reading) to be a simple issue that allows the participants to make a decision after limited discussion. This sets the tone for the rest of the meeting's action and engages individuals right away in the business at hand. After you have dealt with a few simple items, tackle the harder issues on the agenda. If difficult matters are left until the end of the meeting when individuals are tired, the discussion will be less productive and possibly even more contentious. However, there are times when it is better to place a hard issue at the end of a meeting. If it is a topic that you don't think should have much dialogue or could be unnecessarily contentious, then placing it at the end can be a wise move. Participants still have the opportunity to speak, but they will often be less verbose.

Get to know *Robert's Rules of Order*.[1] In large meetings, *Robert's Rules of Order* is almost essential for order and agreement. While small meetings don't usually necessitate the rigid order of *Robert's Rules*, it can be helpful when a decision needs to be made. For example, a discussion on a particular item extends for a long period of time as everyone in the room weighs in on the topic at hand. Intense dialogue has taken place, but no decision has materialized. In this situation, suggesting that someone make a motion provides an actual opportunity for a decision to occur. This also helps to halt the continued pontification of opinions that have already been mentioned three or four times. A good leader knows *Robert's Rules* and when to implement them.

If you are the leader of the meeting, then lead. Meetings become tedious, long, unruly, and unproductive when the leader does not lead. This doesn't mean you need to be dictatorial, but it does mean that those in the room need to know that you are leading. Express your opinion, come with an agenda, and be willing to correct errors in the conversation. However, you also need to know how to listen, when to allow others to take control of a conversation, when and if it is necessary to be more directive, and when it is better to allow the group to find its own way on a particular issue.

If a meeting is getting "bogged down" with an agenda item, don't be afraid to be creative. When a difficult motion would benefit from more discussion or concerted prayer, then table the agenda item until the next meeting. A good meeting leader also knows when to move a contentious or weighty item to a subcommittee; ask for a report to the larger body with a recommendation. Smaller groups allow for simplified and often more helpful discussions.

Don't always insist on your own way. As a leader, lead, but don't demand. While you may serve as the leader, chairman, or moderator, multiple people are involved—and for good reason. Lead the meeting, but do so humbly.

As a pastor, you will constantly lead meetings. Over time you will become more adept and able by experience. In the meantime, attempt to apply some of the advice outlined above and implement what is helpful.

PART 4

PITFALLS *of* YOUNG PASTORS

32

Beginning Too Fast

Better is the end of a thing than its beginning,
and the patient in spirit is better than the
proud in spirit.

Ecclesiastes 7:8

A young man sets off to his first pastorate after completing years of theological study. He has sent out résumés, endured interviews, waded through ordination exams, and waited anxiously for a church to call and say, "We want you to be our pastor." He packs up the U-Haul with his books sealed in boxes and heads across the country, ready to begin pastoring. Where should he start? What should he do?

Many wonderful matters call for his attention: he desires to institute a more helpful Sunday school curriculum, launch a systematic overhaul of the diaconate, engage the community in a new way, equip the elders to shepherd, implement a new order of worship, encourage the congregation to embrace church planting—and the list goes on. He believes the Lord gave him a vision for the church, and he knows where it needs to go. However, it is at this point that a wise visionary will apply the brakes. He cannot and should not run through the church as the proverbial bull in a china shop.

Dear pastor, start slow. Exercise self-control in what you seek to implement. Get to know your people, and learn the dynamics in the church. See yourself as a student rather than as a teacher, and take your time; don't launch new initiatives in the first six months. This approach will pay dividends in the long run. Invite families over for dinner and ask important questions about their lives and the life of the church. Make pastoral visits to the homes of your new flock. Explore their struggles, recognize their sins, identify their gifts, and discover their passions. Use those early weeks to invest in the elders and deacons. Discover the next generation of leadership waiting in the wings. Identify the church matriarch or patriarch so that you are prepared to handle discussions and initiatives down the road. Above all, allow the church time to get to know you. They want to follow you as a leader or they wouldn't have called you. That being said, relationships need time and opportunity to develop trust.

I encourage new pastors to begin by preaching through a small book of the Bible (such as Ruth, Jonah, Philippians, or

Colossians). Refrain from launching into a three-year campaign of Isaiah's sixty-six chapters. Diving into a long book can be hard for even the most seasoned congregations who know and trust their pastor. They will appreciate hearing you preach from a few different books and genres. At the start, shy away from books with hard passages or difficult central messages. Pick a book like Philippians or Colossians that affords the opportunity to encourage the congregation and easily set Christ before them. There is something to be said for allowing the congregation to get to know you and you to know them before you address them about suffering (1 Peter), contentious issues within the church (1 Corinthians), the justice of God (Judges), and the dangers of false teachers (1 Timothy). They will hear these lessons better from a man they know loves them—someone they have grown to respect.

Starting slow isn't a lack of leadership; it's leadership in action. Get to know your people and give them the opportunity to get to know you. Then boldly lead them in the vision you and the elders of the church believe God has given.

33

Idealistic Zeal

Desire without knowledge is not good,
and whoever makes haste with his feet
misses his way.

Proverbs 19:2

One of the things I most appreciate about young pastors
is their zeal. Zeal inspires, motivates, and encourages.
However, it can also cause significant turmoil. While good in its
place, zeal should not serve as your guiding light. Knowledge,
pastoral sensitivity, and patience necessarily temper, direct,
and shape zeal for a purposeful end.

Most young pastors think they know more than they do. That may sound harsh, but I have found it to be universally true—and I speak from personal experience. Almost all pastors look back and wish they could have restrained the young man they once were. Be careful what hills you decide to die on. Some issues that I thought were extremely important in my early ministry I no longer give the same weight. In the beginning, you don't possess the knowledge you will one day have. I am not inferring that you should shy away from leading, implementing, or teaching the things you are passionate about. Just be willing to be teachable and learn from those around you. The doctrine, practice, or conviction that seems essential at the start may not be as necessary as you think it is. Yes, you have been called by the Lord to instruct and teach the people under your care, but are you also teachable? Are you willing to listen to more seasoned pastors in the area, as well as your elders and members of the congregation? They are trying to temper, not destroy, your zeal.

Zeal often manifests itself in an idealistic mind-set. I look back on my first pastorate and think of the difficulty I brought to that church with a decision I made that was motivated by zeal. A little pastoral sensitivity would have gone a long way, but at the time I was convinced that it was good for children to be in the corporate worship services of the church. I still hold to that conviction. However, I was idealistic and not pastorally sensitive as I sought to implement this change in a church that had never included elementary-age children in its worship services. I proceeded to teach and convince the elders of the necessity of this practice; once they were on board, I sent a letter to the congregation informing them of the impending change in practice. We led one open meeting with the congregation so that parents could ask questions about having their children in worship. I remember some parents expressing concern, but I charged ahead in my zeal without sensitivity. Did it destroy the church? No. But a number of families were not ready for such an abrupt change, and it was a difficult season for them. Some of them even chose not to remain at the church. Looking back, I wish I had taken more time and listened more closely to their concerns.

Be patient with others. Be flexible when setting goals and time frames. Be patient in seeing vision realized. Zeal often pushes and demands immediate realization. Let that zeal shine, but keep it reined in. Allow it to be corralled, slowed down, and tempered. Looking back, you will be thankful, and in the meantime, your people will be grateful.

34

Discouragement

The kingdom of God is as if a man should scatter seed
on the ground. He sleeps and rises night and day, and
the seed sprouts and grows; he knows not how.

Mark 4:26–27

Pastoring is an odd endeavor. A carpenter comes to the end of his day, looks back on his work, sees the fruit of it, and goes home with some satisfaction. A doctor, a librarian, a writer, a secretary, a stockbroker, and almost every other professional can do the same thing. Pastors are different. We come to the end of the day and don't quite know what we accomplished. We labor in the spiritual realm and are called to be physicians of the soul. We minister the Word, pray, counsel, disciple, teach, preach, and evangelize, but seldom do these efforts produce immediate and concrete "results" that prove our labor was beneficial and effectual. Evidence of our hard work is sometimes impossible to see, which can be discouraging. How do we combat this?

We must remind ourselves that we can't rely on what we see or don't see as evidence of a day well spent in ministry: "For we do not wrestle against flesh and blood" (Eph. 6:12). Please don't misunderstand me. Over the course of our ministries and in the life of the church, we should expect to see fruitfulness. A man who never sees fruit from his labors among the people of God may not possess the gifts he thinks he does. But we should not expect to know, as a merchant does, what the net result of our daily activity has been.

In this situation, we may find ourselves tempted to "produce" as a way to alleviate our discouragement. Wanting to be able to show what we have accomplished can be a trap. When I come home in the evening and my wife inquires, "What did you do today?" it can be hard to say, "I studied and prayed." It becomes even more difficult when an elder, congregant, or fellow staff member asks the question. We want to demonstrate something, to hold up a tangible sign of our hard work. As a result, we schedule too many meetings and direct our energy toward producing policies, generating emails, assigning tasks, making phone calls, and focusing on numbers of attendance and giving. In short, we immerse ourselves in administrative tasks because of our insipient desire to show others (and ourselves) what we have accomplished today, this week, or this month. All the while, the work that God called us to begins to fade into the background. Don't fall into this trap!

Though the invisible nature of our work can be discouraging at times, it also serves as one of the most encouraging aspects of gospel ministry. We never quite know what the Lord is doing or has done. A conversation we thought meaningless leads an individual to conversion; a poor sermon shakes a sinner from their stupor; weeks of agonizing and apparently ineffective prayer lead to an answer months later. God calls us to spiritual work, and we don't always see what is happening. We must remember that our calling is simply to be faithful in what he has called us to and to use the means he has appointed. He does the rest.

The parable of the growing seed in Mark 4:26–29 demonstrates this reality. The farmer goes out, scatters seed on the ground, and then retires to sleep. His labor is the spreading of the seed. That is his task. If he is looking for immediate gratification for a day's hard work, he will find none. He must lay down to rest; while he sleeps, the Lord works. When he awakes he finds the Lord blessed the seed and produced a rich harvest. A farmer who goes to bed discouraged because he doesn't see fruit immediately after planting the seed is a fool. Farming doesn't work that way—and neither does pastoring. We sow; he produces the harvest.

Dear pastor, be faithful during the light of day and go home with a peaceful conscience. Enjoy a good night's sleep and wake in the morning to begin again. The Lord is worthy of our trust. Do not be discouraged; he is at work.

Taking Yourself Too Seriously

Substituting Self for Christ

For I decided to know nothing among you except Jesus Christ and him crucified.

1 Corinthians 2:2

My wife took me aside one evening and said, "You are not what they need." She spoke the right words at the right time. I had spent months trying to assist a couple in the midst of their marital conflict and rampant drug abuse. My phone would ring late at night and early in the morning. There were often tears and sometimes even yelling on the other end of the phone. On multiple occasions, I dropped everything to run out the door, drive across town, and minister to this struggling couple. In truth, I loved them and wanted to see them safely in the arms of Christ. However, as I look back, I also thought too much of my own ability to change them. My wife was right: I wasn't what they needed. They knew that if they called, I would jump. Unfortunately, amid all of my zeal to help them, I had conditioned them to turn to me for all their answers. While ministering to them in the name of Christ, I was turning them away from Christ.

Pastors, don't take yourselves too seriously. We often maintain a view of ourselves that supersedes reality, but we are not indispensable. We are critical, but we are not essential. Christ alone is indispensable and essential. The apostle Paul sets a good example: "For I decided to know nothing among you except Jesus Christ and him crucified" (1 Cor. 2:2). This statement helps us to comprehend why he became so incensed by the division in the Corinthian church. Some said, "I follow Paul," or "I follow Apollos," or "I follow Cephas" (1 Cor. 1:12). We serve as pastors—not saviors, messiahs, or christs. In the midst of ministry it is easy to cross the line in the name of helping others. However, "There is one mediator between God and men, the man Christ Jesus" (1 Tim. 2:5).

We must be careful that the wrong kind of culture doesn't develop around our ministry. We should not desire sycophants, fans, or enthusiasts. If people join the church because of us rather than Christ, there's a problem. If individuals speak to their friends about us rather than Christ, we ought to grieve over the insult. The pastor who doesn't take himself too seriously contentedly preaches Christ and him crucified. He doesn't need his ego stroked, his name known, or his due given in this life. Rather, he confesses with John the Baptist, "He must increase, but I must decrease" (John 3:30).

A humble pastor is a good pastor. By not taking yourself too seriously, you provide fertile soil for the growth of humility not only in pastoring but also in your entire Christian life. A humble man seeking to serve the Lord is a man who is already rightly seeking and serving the Lord. Let us not take ourselves too seriously.

|||||||||||||

36

Not Taking Yourself
Seriously Enough

Do not neglect the gift you have, which was given you
by prophecy when the council of elders laid their hands
on you. Practice these things, immerse yourself in them,
so that all may see your progress.

1 Timothy 4:14–15

Those residing in the Western Hemisphere in previous
generations tended to respect and even admire men in
the pastorate, but those days, generally speaking, have passed.
Unfortunately, many men in the pastorate today also evidence
a low opinion of their calling, as demonstrated by their lack of

seriousness. While pastors certainly don't need to be prudish or take on the role of the proverbial stick-in-the-mud (it always helps to have a good sense of humor and an affable personality in the ministry), pastors should also take themselves seriously. Our calling demands it.

We live our lives in the public eye. We are to be "above reproach," "sober-minded," "self-controlled," and "respectable" (1 Tim. 3:2). Not only are we to be respectable in the family of God, but we are also "to be well thought of by outsiders" (1 Tim. 3:7). Others are to see our progress in the faith (1 Tim. 4:15). A pastor not being attentive to his own life can adversely affect the spirituality of an entire congregation and community.

We need to tend our congregations with a serious resolve. The author of Hebrews writes to the church, "Obey your leaders and submit to them, for they are keeping watch over your souls, as those who will have to give an account" (Heb. 13:17). As pastors, we must give an account of the church to the Lord concerning those he has placed under our care. This is a significant calling. There is nothing trivial about ministry. What we do week in and week out either benefits or hurts the Lord's sheep. Our lives are spent either faithfully serving the kingdom or neglecting it.

Resist the temptation to simply go through the motions. Monday comes, and we have the same deadlines that filled the week before. A staff meeting takes place Monday afternoon, and Wednesday's schedule includes putting together the order of worship and meeting with the elders. The sermon notes must be completed by Thursday, the Sunday school lesson organized by Friday, and the sermon drafted by Friday evening. All the while we attempt to fit in pastoral visits, counseling appointments, and administration. Too easily, it becomes routine to check off the boxes, punch the time clock, and accomplish the tasks the church pays us to do. May it never be! Our calling demands more than going through the motions. As pastors, we are charged with reaching out with the truth of the gospel to others, with ministering to their languishing, dying, and overburdened souls. This is a serious calling.

Therefore, we cannot treat lightly our doctrine, spiritual lives, reputation, time, efforts, preparation, leadership, marriages, children, preaching, teaching, praying, hospitality, discipling, and recreation. We must take our entire life seriously, diligently seeking to be good stewards of what he has graciously entrusted to us. Even as we attempt to not take ourselves too seriously (as the previous chapter discussed), we must also refrain from not taking ourselves seriously enough. It can be deadly for our people, our ministries, and our souls.

37

Here We Go Again

Theological Hobbyhorses

Therefore I testify to you this day that I am innocent
of the blood of all, for I did not shrink from declaring
to you the whole counsel of God.

Acts 20:26–27

Most presbytery meetings include the examination of some young man for the pastoral ministry. Part of the examination includes the preaching of a sermon before all of the pastors who are present. I remember sitting at my first presbytery meeting. A young man ascended the stairs, entered the pulpit, and began to preach his ordination sermon before a host of seasoned pastors. Obviously nervous, he began his sermon by saying with a shaking voice, "My text this morning is Ephesians 1." In response, I heard one seasoned Presbyterian pastor say to another in a low whisper, "Surprise, surprise!" and they chuckled. Young Presbyterian pastors aren't hard to spot. They carry a Bible in one hand and a Westminster Confession of Faith in the other; dressed in a suit coat, their topic of conversation is usually the doctrine of predestination (I can laugh, because I am one of them). Ephesians 1 is a popular text for young Presbyterians. Sometimes it feels like their only text.

Pastors tend to have theological hobbyhorses. They love the doctrines of grace or six-day creation or baptism, and everyone knows it. You don't have to spend much time around them to discover their passions. They will tell you, and if you are still listening, they will tell you again. They seemingly find a way in every conversation, sermon, and teaching opportunity to bridge the gap to their topic of choice. Like a circus act that gets old because the pony keeps doing the same trick, the pastor who seems to talk only about one thing can expect people to begin to turn a deaf ear. Be passionate about your convictions according to Scripture. Don't shy away from sharing them, but don't play only one tune on your fiddle. People will stop considering it a tune worth hearing.

Preaching *lectio continua* expository sermons safeguards the young pastor from this tendency. *Lectio continua* is the Latin term for "continuous reading." It boasts a long history in the Christian church and refers to preaching consecutively through one book of the Bible. When finished with that book, the preacher moves on to another. This prevents the pastor from topical preaching, which tends to find its way back to his favorite theological subject. There are seasons and occasions for a topical sermon series, but these should be less common than they are in most churches today. Even in a sermon series, the content should be expository; the sermon should flow from the text and not from the pastor's creativity. Expository *lectio continua* preaching serves as one of the best safeguards against saddling that old, trusty hobbyhorse with yet another sermon.

It is also important to seek regular feedback about your preaching and teaching ministry. If you have a staff team, meet with them on Monday or Tuesday morning to review the worship service. Ask them to give honest feedback about your sermon, and reflect on it.

Listen to the people of your congregation as well. They will approach you with questions and comments about things they think interest you. They will often pick up on your passions and emphasis in your preaching. This can provide an excellent barometer of the depth and breadth of your preaching, teaching, and leadership in ministry.

It's not wrong or even harmful to be passionate about one discipline or area of theology or practice. However, it can be wrong and harmful to be *too* passionate about it—passionate to the point that everyone knows what you are going to say and your entire ministry is shaped by it. Don't ride that theological hobbyhorse until she is only a beaten-up nag that no one pays any attention to. Give your people "the whole counsel of God" (Acts 20:27).

38

Giraffe Syndrome

Lack of Contentment

You keep him in perfect peace
whose mind is stayed on you,
because he trusts in you.

Isaiah 26:3

It is subtle but destructive. It creeps in before a pastor is aware, seizing and dashing his effectiveness, his zeal, his passion, and his ministry. I call it "giraffe syndrome." It is the temptation to have one's head swiveling about, neck outstretched and craning to see another part of the vineyard, wishing he were there. In essence, it is a lack of contentment. Instead of attending to the ministry before us, with the people given to us, we begin to desire something else—usually something bigger, easier, or more pronounced. Sometimes we will focus on *anything* else, just as long as it's different.

At times the Lord makes us restless and gently prods us to move to another field of labor in the kingdom. This happens to most ministers at some point in their ministry and is a holy discontentment; but this chapter is not addressing that issue. Rather, I am speaking about the discontentment that affects a man not because the Lord is prodding him to move on but because he is too busy looking in other places. Anytime we sense discontent in ourselves, we must test it. Is it holy or unholy? Unholy discontentment is an enemy we should flee.

The pitfall of discontentment primarily falls into three categories. The first is a lack of contentment with *where* you are called to serve, which begins with a series of insidious thoughts: *The church over there has more resources. That part of the country is more appealing. If only I could have a support staff like that church.* Subtly, maybe even in a way imperceptible to others, our heart's affection for our local church diminishes (Exod. 20:17). When discontentment takes hold, faithfulness usually fades. We would never say it and would be slow to acknowledge it, but we don't strive like we once did; we don't labor quite as hard, pray as fervently, or prepare as well.

Discontentment destroys. My dear friends in the ministry, be content where you are. The Lord has called you to this church, this city, and this field of labor until he clearly calls you somewhere else. You are his man for this place. You may think that others can do it—and no doubt there are others who can—but he has called you here for a specific purpose. You may not know why, but he does. He is the Lord of the church, and you serve at his call. Be faithful where you are.

The second category is a lack of contentment with *whom* you are called to serve. I had this reality impressed on me a number of years ago when I labored as a church planter. It was about a year into the church plant, and I was busy trying to connect with people in the community. However, the people the Lord brought across my path were not the kind of people I expected or was seeking. On one particular morning, I had just left a counseling session with a man who had abused his wife and was facing the ramifications. I was driving across town to meet with another man I was counseling who had neglected his children. En route, I returned a phone call to a weeping woman whose husband was an alcoholic. I hung up the phone and, to my shame, uttered out loud in frustration, "Lord, just give me some normal people to serve," as if these people weren't "normal."

The moment the words came out of my mouth, I was struck with grief. "What comes out of the mouth proceeds from the heart" (Matt. 15:18); and my heart was not in a good place. Oh, how it grieved me that I wanted "other people" when the Lord had granted me the privilege and honor to serve these particular individuals in gospel ministry. These people needed gospel truth, but I was busy making my own plans and thought it would be better to start a church with more "stable" people. God had given me these broken, hurting, battered people. To my shame, I was not loving them or serving Christ well.

Whoever he has drawn together in your local church, he wants you to serve. Not only are they to be your "glory and joy" (1 Thess. 2:20), but you are also to serve them with joy. The writer of Hebrews says of leaders in the church, "Let them do this with joy and not with groaning, for that would be of no advantage to you" (Heb. 13:17). He wants you to reach the people in your community and serve the people in your church—no matter how difficult, broken, offensive, or unlike the demographic you imagine yourself ministering to (Matt. 9:10–13).

The third category is a lack of contentment with *how* you are called to serve. Too many pastors desire to be conference speakers, writers, and seminary professors more than they want to pastor their local church. It is the rare pastor who should preach regularly outside his own church's walls. While it is the call of some men to do so, their numbers are few. We need fewer aspiring conference speakers and more faithful pastors committed to their local churches.

Be content with *where* you are called to serve, *whom* you are called to serve, and *how* you are called to serve; "godliness with contentment is great gain" (1 Tim. 6:6). Pursue contentment. Pray for it and embrace it; find your rest there.

39

One Size Fits All

For though by this time you ought to be teachers, you need someone to teach you again the basic principles of the oracles of God. You need milk, not solid food.

Hebrews 5:12

Refrain from doing ministry exclusively through your own grid. I define "grid" as the life experiences, personal struggles, and future hopes that shape our spiritual lives, our reception of the Word, and our ministries. Be aware of your grid and don't diagnose every issue, craft each sermon, or write every newsletter exclusively through this lens.

The Scriptures are varied, and the truth in them is multi-faceted. Don't neglect this reality; it should lead your ministry to be dynamic rather than static. Our focus can and should be adjusted depending on the person, situation, and need. Every hospital visit does not require the same reading of Scripture. There are times that an individual in the hospital needs to be reminded of the watchful care of the Lord, so the pastor might read Psalm 121. At other times an individual may be consumed with anxiety, so the pastor could turn to Matthew 6. However, there are yet other times the patient in the hospital may need a gentle rebuke for being consumed with the things of this world, so the pastor could read from 1 John 2:15–17.

Our own limited grid encroaches most pervasively in the pulpit. Some men preach the same sermon every week; only the text varies. Their sermons ring with predictability, and their applications grow stale as their people stagnate. Unfortunately, this situation often escapes the pastor's notice. Those who hunger for more sustenance may raise an objection, but if they feel their objections have fallen on deaf ears, they will likely leave the church, unsatisfied. The remaining members of the congregation may offer no complaints because they find the sermons palatable and comforting. They hear nothing new, and their pet sins are seldom disrupted. If your sermons never rankle and are always considered pleasant by the people in the pew, this may be a sign that your preaching has become singularly focused.

If we enter the pulpit believing everyone needs the same message all of the time, the people under our care live in great danger. If there is only one medicine we have for every ill, many of our people will leave unaffected. If we persist without variation in our approach and message, our people will suffer. Please do not misunderstand me. Are we to preach the gospel every week? Of course! But don't rob the gospel of its multifaceted application and complexity. It is simple and yet incredibly complex. The Scriptures do not repeat one line over and over. Neither do they state one application again and again in different ways. They minister to the entire person, they minister to every person, and they minister to every need.

Your congregation will include the weary and those struggling with guilt, fear, anxiety, and depression. But it will also consist of the proud, the arrogant, the sluggard, and the idle. It will include people pleasers and people haters. It will harbor skeptics and zealots. You will minister to those who have suffered greatly and others who have barely suffered. Some will operate rationally and others emotionally. Some will exhibit sensitivity and others will seem rock hard. Vary your ministry, especially your preaching, to reach each and every type of person under your care. This means altering your message, addressing applications to different types of people, structuring church programs to engage diverse groups, preaching from various genres in the Scripture, recommending sundry categories of books from the pulpit, and maintaining flexibility in how you minister to individuals in pastoral visits, hospital rooms, and counseling opportunities. The Lord has fashioned you as a physician of the soul, so seek to administer the right balm in the right way with the right dosage.

One of the beauties of the Scriptures is that there is no person, no sin, and no struggle on the face of the earth they don't address. Scripture can be applied as a balm or a sword (Heb. 4:12). It can be useful for correction or training in righteousness (2 Tim. 3:16). It can be sweet (Ps. 119:103), or it can be hard (John 6:66). Allow the Scriptures to shine forth in all their glory, in all their ways, to every type of person in every conceivable circumstance.

40

Devastated by People

For Demas, in love with this present world, has deserted
me and gone to Thessalonica.

2 Timothy 4:10

People are essential to pastoral ministry. They can be wonderful, encouraging, supportive, and refreshing (Philem.
7). However, they can also be fickle, discouraging, and dam-
aging. As a pastor, you will see both of these realities clearly
and continually. One of the hardest things about ministry is
the disappointment we experience as a result of other people.

It is right to be disappointed by the actions and decisions of
some of the people under our care. I look back over a decade

of ministry and think of a man I believed had come to saving faith but who now rejects Christ entirely. I am discouraged as I think of someone I counted as a dear friend in the church who committed an act of incredible betrayal. I remember a woman whom the church ministered to with great resolve and dedication who now slanders that same church. I think of those who left the church over petty disagreements, an elder who fell into a life of adultery, and a family converted to a different religion. Ministry yields many opportunities for disappointment. Amid all of this sorrow, guard against being devastated by people.

When I reflect on this temptation, I think of Demas and Paul. Demas was one of the members of Paul's inner circle. In Philemon, Paul lists him in his final farewell with the likes of Epaphras, Mark, Aristarchus, and Luke (Philem. 1:23). Paul mentions him again in the farewell of the book of Colossians (Col. 4:14). Paul must have trusted Demas to include him in these lists of venerable saints, yet we turn to 2 Timothy 4:10 and read, "For Demas, in love with the present world, has deserted me and gone to Thessalonica." This man that Paul trusted and counted on as a dear brother in Christ betrayed him. Even more than that, Demas betrayed the Lord. He turned his back on the faith for love of the world.

Demas's defection could have devastated Paul, but he didn't allow it. If he had, he would have been distracted from the ministry before him, and we would have all suffered as a result. No doubt Paul grieved, lamented, and prayed for Demas, but he did not allow one man's damning decision to sidetrack or sideline his ministry.

Individuals will disappoint us over the course of our ministries. That is a guarantee. The world and sin exercise a strong pull, and some of the people we love the most will disappoint us the most. Men and women we trust will prove untrustworthy. People in whom we thought faith had taken hold will turn out to be like the seed thrown on rocky ground (Mark 4:5–6). Some we thought were mature will prove to be only infants (1 Cor. 3:1). Allow yourself to grieve, struggle with disappointment, and even wrestle with discouragement—but don't allow yourself to be devastated. If you do, our adversary will have secured two victories instead of one.

41

Lecture Sermons

For since, in the wisdom of God, the world did not know
God through wisdom, it pleased God through the folly
of what we preach to save those who believe.

1 Corinthians 1:21

A preacher in his late forties once told me, "I am as good of a preacher as I will ever be." This man still had another fifteen-plus years of public preaching ministry before him. I certainly hope he hadn't already reached his apex as a preacher. By God's grace, we want to continually grow as communicators of God's Word. Whether in our exposition, mannerisms, voice control, theology, applications, illustrations, structure, or connection with the congregation, we can all mature as preachers. As one would expect, most young preachers have a lot of room for growth, and they seem especially prone to giving dry lectures rather than life-changing sermons.

In some ways, I am encouraged when I hear a young preacher give a dry lecture. It usually means that he is committed to expositional preaching. His engagement with the grammar, syntax, and original languages is clearly demonstrated in the pulpit. Thank God for young pastors who are committed to such study and maintain such a high view of the inerrant Word of God. Yet, as much as I am thankful for such a commitment, dry lectures do not belong in the pulpit.

Lectures are not preaching just as commentary on a passage is not preaching. We are not downloading information or conducting an informational seminar when we preach. Good preaching aims to reach the affections through the mind. Unfortunately, lecture sermons aim purely at the mind with no concern for engaging the affections of the congregation. A sound preacher will learn the marked difference in these two approaches. I define effective preaching as the proclamation of biblical truth with passion, which is aimed at the affections of the people listening as they engage the truth of the text with their minds by the stirring of the Holy Spirit.

Young preachers' sermons too often lack passion. As Richard Baxter pointedly states, "I preach'd as never sure to preach again, and as a dying man to dying men."[1] We are handling eternal truths, and lives are weighed in the balance. The pulpit is not the place for passionless pontificating. People do not need theatrics or unnecessary drama, and neither of these has any place in good preaching. Rather, pastors need to be filled with love for the person in the pew—a love that manifests itself in passionate pleading. David Hume, an unbeliever, was asked once why he went to listen to George Whitefield, especially since Hume personally didn't believe the gospel. Hume reportedly responded, "I don't believe it, but he does." A pastor gripped by the truth of the Word he preaches will reflect it in the pulpit. This type of preacher serves as a ready conduit; the people listening are likely to be gripped by that same truth.

Listen to good expositional preachers and study how they preach a text's meaning in a way that engages the listener. You will notice that an experienced preacher often uses engaging illustrations and challenging applications. Young pastor, spend time working on illustrations. They shouldn't dominate a sermon, but neither should they be absent. In the same way, labor diligently to draw helpful applications from the passage. Aim for applications of the text that are as rich as the theological truth you are trying to communicate. As you seek to apply the Word of God, target different types of people in various circumstances. No sermon will affect every person, but over the course of time your sermons should minister to the proud, the fearful, the lonely, the doubting, the lost, the worldly, the afflicted, the skeptical, and the growing among you.

Remember your commentaries; likewise, Greek and Hebrew serve as useful tools, but they are tools. Like a good spade and pickax, they assist in bringing the jewel to the surface. They are not the jewel itself and should never be on display.

Unfortunately, many congregations find themselves subjected to a technical commentary on the passage each week rather than a sermon. People in the pew seldom benefit from a pastor displaying his knowledge of Greek or Hebrew. It is the odd parishioner who will find his or her heart stirred by learning the intricacies of the subjective genitive. Aspire not to impress but rather to see Christ and his truth impressed on their hearts.

As a final thought, let me leave you with these words from Jonathan Edwards:

> It does not answer the aim which God had in this institution, merely for men to have good commentaries and expositions on the Scripture, and other good books of divinity; because, although these may tend, as well as preaching, to give a good doctrinal or speculative understanding of the word of God, yet they have not an equal tendency to impress them on men's hearts and affections. God hath appointed a particular and lively application of his word, in the preaching of it, as a fit means to affect sinners with the importance of religion, their own misery, the necessity of a remedy, and the glory and sufficiency of a remedy provided; to stir up the pure minds of the saints, quicken their affections by often bringing the great things of religion in their remembrance, and setting them in their proper colours, though they know them, and have been fully instructed in them already.[2]

42

Illustrations and Applications Gone Awry

If we put bits into the mouths of horses so that they obey us, we guide their whole bodies as well. Look at the ships also: though they are so large and are driven by strong winds, they are guided by a very small rudder wherever the will of the pilot directs. So also the tongue is a small member, yet it boasts of great things.

James 3:3–5

As discussed in the previous chapter, engaging illustrations and challenging applications often mark excellent sermons. However, if not used well, illustrations and applications distract rather than aid. They can dominate a sermon, lead people astray, or frustrate the listener. There is a real art to finding the right illustrations and applications.

Vary your illustrations. Some will be short and sweet. Others should last a little longer in order to allow the listener to engage more thoroughly. The illustrations also need to vary in topic. Most preachers are more comfortable giving illustrations from a certain genre or sphere of life. For example, I love history and sports; thankfully, history and sports lend themselves well to illustrations. However, I can't use them for every illustration I give. If I do, people with little interest in history and sports may grow tired of my preaching (and I don't need to give them any other reasons to do that).

Illustrations also go awry when they center too often on the preacher. Sometimes focusing on yourself can distract the listener from the text by turning their attention to you. Furthermore, when giving illustrations that include you or your family members, don't always assume the role of the hero. Pastors who tend to illustrate in this way sound more like someone on a public relations tour than a servant pointing people to Christ. From experience, let me encourage you not to use your wife as a sermon illustration unless she has agreed beforehand. Likewise, your children will provide many opportunities for illustrations, but choose wisely. It is easier when they are young, but as they grow older you need to consider whether it is appropriate to use their triumphs, foibles, and silliness as illustrations. Don't overlook the narrative portions of Scripture and nature itself when looking for inspiration; much insightful and illustrative material can be gleaned from them.

Most importantly, don't allow illustrations to become the meat of your sermons. Illustrations should never overshadow the text. Frankly, some illustrations are just too good. They engage the person in the pew too much and become the focal point of the sermon. This makes for good public speaking but not good preaching. On the other hand, some illustrations dominate the sermon because they are so bad. Their inappropriateness sticks in the minds of people, making it difficult to move past them. We serve as preachers of the Word. If the average person in the pew walks away from the service laughing, crying, or scratching their head about an illustration but not remembering the message of the text, we have failed.

Applications can also quickly go awry. When applying the text, approach it in different ways. Sometimes the applications work best scattered throughout the sermon. At other times it may suit the sermon better to close with a few applications. Mix it up so it doesn't feel the same every week. Otherwise your applications become too predictable. Allow for general and specific applications. General applications put the onus on the listener to think through personal implications. For example, "Parents, we have been charged by God to raise our children to know the truth of the Scriptures, so do not neglect teaching them these great truths." However, it is also necessary to provide a steady dose of specific applications that help your people navigate the road from the text to daily life. For example, "Parents, we have been charged by God to raise our children to know the truth of the Scriptures. One of the best ways of doing this is to practice family worship at home. Lead your children in reading the Scriptures and praying daily."

As you think through how to apply the text, keep different groups of people in mind. It is impossible to speak to every sin, struggle, or need every week, but over the course of months, your applications should knock on the door of every heart. Be careful with radical and far-reaching applications such as, "We are to be heavenly minded, so think more about heaven than you do the things of earth." Though this statement contains truth, it lacks nuance and specificity. These kinds of applications can pile a lot of guilt on those listening. Ask older, wiser, and more experienced Christians whether your applications tend to wander in this way. Above all, preach appropriate applications from the text. It is a shame when a preacher does a wonderful job of exegeting the passage and then applies something foreign to the text (usually of his own making).

Good sermons consist of sound biblical and theological thought. Engaging illustrations and challenging applications transform good sermons into great sermons. A faithful preacher will take time to find both, and his people will receive the blessing.

||||||||||||

43

Iron Grip

Holding People Too Tightly

And if anyone will not receive you or listen to your words, shake off the dust from your feet when you leave that house or town.

Matthew 10:14

Letting people go proves to be one of the hardest aspects of ministry. Most of us became pastors because we believe in the efficacy of God's Word and the need to preach this truth to others. We know the greatest need of all men, women, and children is the salvation of their souls. Once they come to that saving faith, we pray that they will live in light of it. Therefore, we find it gut-wrenching when someone does not respond to the Word and our ministry as we hoped or thought they would.

Disappointment comes in many forms. It can include the drug-addicted middle-aged man who cannot seem to put his drug use behind him; the selfish and petty husband who listens to our counsel but refuses to change; the homeless man who always greets us with a smile but refuses all help to find a job; the woman who needs help with her rent and is quite willing to accept money from the church but wants no spiritual direction; or the unbeliever who attends church every week, listens to our preaching, loves to meet with us to discuss the sermon, but remains unaffected. Sometimes the examples seem endless.

In such circumstances, idealism can tempt us to hold on to someone too long. No doubt, we must persevere in our ministry to others. Not everyone comes quickly or readily to the truth of Christ. God calls us to pursue sinners and willingly pour out ourselves (Phil. 2:17) for them. No personal sacrifice we make in seeking the salvation of another person's soul is too much. But at times we must "shake the dust from our feet" (Matt. 10:14), stop throwing our "pearls before pigs" (Matt. 7:6), and focus our attention on other people.

This is not an easy decision and should never be taken lightly, but at times it is necessary. Some people will continue to drain your time and efforts as long as you allow them, when others would benefit from that same time and effort. You have only so much energy. "The harvest is plentiful, but the laborers are few" (Luke 10:2). A farmer who works the same field time and again but reaps no harvest while the field one furlong over would reap a bountiful harvest is not wisely spending his time.

Minister to all kinds of people, but don't hold any one person too tightly. We must let some people go. Weigh the matter in prayer, seek the peace of the Lord, and persevere as long as it is wise—but when you are clearly "spinning your wheels," move on. While this may be difficult, it is necessary, and there is nothing unfaithful about it. Many people around you need eternal truth. "Lift up your eyes, and see that the fields are white for harvest" (John 4:35). Go reach them for the glory of God.

||||||||||

44

Pastor Envy

Some indeed preach Christ from envy and rivalry, but others from good will.

Philippians 1:15

Television, the internet, the publishing industry, podcasts, and radio have made pastors today more aware of other pastors than at any other time in the history of the church. What should be a positive situation, however, often becomes a negative one. Instead of rejoicing and thanking God for the ministry and gifts of others, jealousy, pride, and envy take over. Surely few things grieve our Lord more than those who "preach Christ from envy and rivalry" (Phil. 1:15), and we must continually be on guard against this enemy. Envy deadens the soul and steals the joy, fruit, and aim of ministry like nothing else.

We need to discipline our minds to ward off this adversary. As you seek to do so, pursue thankfulness and gratitude, for they hail as the great vanquishers of envy. Remind yourself often of the blessings you enjoy. Though not perfect, the congregation you serve surpasses anything you warrant. The privilege of preaching to these people is an honor that outstrips the greatest commendation you could receive on earth; certainly the opportunities before you eclipse your natural abilities. Remember that you deserve nothing and that God has given all things generously. Thankfulness and gratitude should be your constant companions.

Quickly repent when a thought of envy or jealousy enters your mind. Pray and thank God for the gifts or ministry that he has given the individual your heart envies. Praying for other pastors and their success lays the groundwork of rejoicing for them instead of coveting what they have or do.

Remind yourself often that you are serving where the Lord would have you and it is more than enough. Has he called you to minister to a handful of people? My friends, there is plenty of labor to keep you busy for a lifetime. If you count your ministry as small, then be "faithful over a little" (Matt. 25:21). That is your duty and obligation. It should also be your joy.

Pastor envy knows no end but destruction. When the pastor of the little country church gains the city church he longed for, the pastor of the even bigger city church becomes the next object of envy. When he pastors the bigger city church, he envies the pastor with the weekly radio sermon broadcast. When he finally convinces his elders to secure airtime for his sermons, he envies the best-selling pastor-author. When he becomes an author, he envies the seminary professor; when a professor, he envies the seminary president.

Envy is never satisfied; it is a continual and deadly pursuit that puts self in the place of Christ. The glory due Christ's name becomes the object of our desire. Before we know it, ministry serves as a means to an end, and the end is the pursuit of earthly glory to the destruction of our eternal glory. Kill envy while it is small; if it is allowed to grow, it will become a monster that consumes everything. May pastor envy never reside in your heart, soul, or mind. Aim for the glory of God and rejoice at the success of the kingdom in every corner, even when it is not your own.

PART 5

JOYS *of* MINISTRY

45

An Eternal Work

For this I toil, struggling with all his energy that he powerfully works within me.

Colossians 1:29

Nothing compares to pastoral ministry. In saying this, I am not denigrating the factory worker, police officer, or doctor. Making cars, maintaining the peace, and healing physical maladies are not to be dismissed as inferior or inconsequential labors. All kinds of work matter. However, pastors bring light to bear where only darkness dwelled. By God's grace, you bring forth life from death through your preaching and ministry. What we do day in, day out has eternal ramifications. There is nothing else like it.

I try to remind myself of two things every day before I pursue the pastoral work before me. First, I labor by the financial tithes of God's people. Therefore, I must strive to honor their sacrifice. Second, I remind myself that I fight in battle every day. By God's calling, "I became a minister according to the stewardship from God that was given to me . . . to make the word of God fully known, the mystery hidden for ages and generations but now revealed to his saints" (Col. 1:25–26). That is my task. I am engaged vocationally in holy warfare every day. Since no day in the pastorate approaches triviality, I am not allowed to "go through the motions."

One senses this resolve in Paul's words when he writes, "Him we proclaim, warning everyone and teaching everyone with all wisdom, that we may present everyone mature in Christ. For this I toil, struggling with all his energy that he powerfully works within me" (Col. 1:28–29). Paul toiled and struggled by the power of God's grace. He wore himself out in gospel ministry. Why? Because the calling demanded his full commitment. What do these momentary and light afflictions matter when we see lives saved from eternal destruction, sin turned back, and people conformed to the image of Christ?

My friends, no greater honor exists in all the earth. Not even the charge of kings, emperors, or presidents rivals our calling. Their thrones, their kingdoms, and their countries do not last, but the throne and kingdom we serve does. Let us every day count the honor and privilege we enjoy as a minister of the gospel. Nothing compares to it—nothing. Some days will be hard, and others will seem impossible, but every night we should go to bed with thanksgiving that God has allowed weak men such as us to labor on the front lines of his eternal kingdom. What a joy! What a privilege!

||||||||||||

46

Confidant

A Trusted Position

Ahithophel was the king's counselor, and Hushai the
Archite was the king's friend.

1 Chronicles 27:33

A couple approached me one Sunday evening after a
worship service and asked whether we could talk
privately. I was happy to do so. I asked my kids to wait for me
quietly in the pew and walked a few feet away with this young
couple. The husband had stopped by my study a few days earlier to tell me his wife was pregnant with their second child.
However, as they approached me on this particular Sunday

evening, they appeared downcast, and tears filled their eyes. Something was clearly wrong. When words finally emerged from the husband's lips, my concern was confirmed. They had experienced a miscarriage that day. Only a few days earlier I had enjoyed the privilege of being one of the few who knew of their pregnancy. But this night the three of us stood hand in hand, and I prayed as they wept in pain and grief.

This is far from a unique day in the life of a pastor. Moments such as these come regularly, which is not to dismiss the importance of this moment in the life of this young couple. Quite the contrary, my eyes brimmed with tears as we talked and prayed. Pastors are weekly, if not daily, given the privilege of entering into the sacred and private experiences of the people under their care—people who seek us out for counsel through good things and hard things. This constitutes part of our calling; it is a high honor and a significant trust.

As I think on this reality, my mind turns to Ahithophel and Hushai in 1 Chronicles. The record shows they maintained a prominent place in the life of King David, and their names are cemented in history because they belonged to his inner circle. One assisted David as a counselor, and the other supported him as a friend. God's people have read about them for millennia because they served as such significant figures in the life of this monumental man.

Few honors exceed that of being the counselor or friend of royalty. Pastors, God grants us the privilege and unique trust of being both a counselor and a friend of royalty. The people we serve are God's children. They are heirs of God and fellow heirs with Christ (Rom. 8:17), and they often seek us out for encouragement, counsel, prayer, confession, and exhortation.

This opportunity should never cease to amaze us. When the knock comes on our study door, the phone rings, or a member of the church pulls us aside on Sunday morning, we enjoy the privilege of entering the inner sanctum of the thoughts, struggles, joys, and temptations of princes and princesses of heaven. Any pastor worth his weight will find this vocational duty humbling and surprising. If not for the truth that we also dwell as children of God and that in him "are hidden all the treasures of wisdom and knowledge" (Col. 2:3), we would be overwhelmed with trepidation at the task before us. But because he has called us to this service and promises to be our counselor (John 14:16) and friend (Luke 7:34), we can rejoice in this godly service (Heb. 13:17). What a privilege God grants to us!

47

We Get Paid for This?

The Privilege of Ministering

What then is my reward? That in my preaching I may present the gospel free of charge, so as not to make full use of my right in the gospel.

1 Corinthians 9:18

I was sitting with a friend at lunch recently, discussing the history of the church. Somehow our conversation turned to the monastic movement in the early church and Middle Ages, of which my friend said (tongue in cheek), "Spending every day brewing ale, baking bread, singing the psalms, praying, and reading the Bible—what isn't there to like?" In the same refrain we could say, "What isn't there to like about gospel ministry?" I know that the labor can be difficult and that sometimes the pressures and disappointments pile up, but we have the privilege of ministering the gospel day in, day out. We must never let this amazing truth become dull in our hearts and minds.

In 1 Corinthians 9, the apostle Paul articulates his right to ask the church to provide income for him. However, at the end of his argument he asks for no such thing. Rather, Paul says that the opportunity to preach the gospel fulfills his great desire. Preaching itself is his reward! There is nothing wrong with receiving a salary for our labors. Paul makes that very point in 1 Corinthians 9:14. In addition, he unreservedly tells Timothy that a laborer deserves his wages (1 Tim. 5:18). Expecting or seeking income is not a problem. However, there is a problem if we miss the crucial fact that our gospel ministry itself is a reward. My friends, God has afforded us one of the greatest gifts in this life. He called us as pastors to serve Christ and his church as undershepherds.

Is there any more noble and glorious task than gospel ministry? We have the joy of devoting our days to studying the Scriptures, praying for the lost, ministering to the hurting, calling the unrepentant to repentance, and preaching the truth of God week in and week out. Who possesses a better calling than we do? No one.

And yet, we can treat our calling as something routine, burdensome, or laborious. If you find yourself stuck in this rut, run to the Lord in prayer. Do not stop, do not hesitate; run!

If weeks of confessing this sin and malaise do not sufficiently revive your soul and zeal for the ministry, then courageously ask your elders for some time off. Not so you may rest on your laurels, but so you may spend concerted time alone with the Lord, asking him to revive your love and passion for his people and your ministry. Most of us experience a season of malaise. While this is normal, it is not to be entertained. We must wage war against it. By God's grace, you will once again delight in your calling to this holy task. As the writer of Hebrews encourages the leaders of the church, "Let them do this with joy and not with groaning, for that would be of no advantage to you" (Heb. 13:17).

Many vocations exist in the world, but none surpass the privilege and honor of the pastorate. The blessings we receive far exceed our efforts. Many of us even receive income for our endeavors. Our days should be filled with joyful thanksgiving.

48

Self-Knowledge

Getting to Know Your Sin and Yourself

Brothers, I do not consider that I have made it my own.
But one thing I do: forgetting what lies behind and strain-
ing forward to what lies ahead, I press on toward the goal
for the prize of the upward call of God in Christ Jesus.
Let those of us who are mature think this way, and if in
anything you think otherwise, God will reveal that also
to you. Only let us hold true to what we have attained.

Philippians 3:13–16

The Puritans maintained that a person must be a student
of both God and one's self before seeking to minister to

others. This is a good rule. We know we need to seek knowledge of God, but we habitually forget that we also need to know ourselves. Here is a promise: if you toil in ministry, you will acquire a distinct and deep knowledge of yourself. It comes with the territory and imparts one of the great blessings of laboring for the gospel.

You will learn your strengths, passions, and gifts as others recognize them and convey their thankfulness for them. By God's grace, you will also see people moved by your exhortations, lives changed through your counseling, saints matured in Christ by your discipleship, and the church ignited with your passion for reaching the lost. This kind of humble encouragement and godly thankfulness rightfully stem from knowing your strengths.

At the same time, you will come to understand your weaknesses and the depth of your own sin. As you study the Word, bend your knees in concerted prayer, and minister to those around you, your own sins will emerge. Our sustained interaction with the Scriptures and spiritual things engages our souls in an exercise of continual self-inspection few others enjoy in this life.

You will also see yourself more clearly through the lens of the people you serve. My wife and I often comment on seeing our own sins present in the lives of our children. Like magnets they pick up our iniquities, and like mirrors they reflect them back to us. Now consider that reality a hundred- or thousand-fold, because congregations tend to reflect their pastors as well. You will observe your weaknesses manifest in them. The sins that have a grip on you will affect the ministry around you, which is one of the scariest realities of pastoral ministry. Yet it also emerges as one of its great encouragements and blessings. As we are brought face-to-face with our own sins, we have the opportunity to repent and seek the Lord's grace. Ultimately, we have the opportunity to grow more in the likeness of our Savior.

We will also begin to perceive ourselves better as we serve on the front lines of this grand spiritual war between the forces of darkness and light. As a pastor, you will be continually engaged in this fight. While all of God's people are constantly waging spiritual battle, our calling makes this an even more intense reality. Our adversary lacks no ignorance in terms of what our sins, our failings, and our corruption could do to a host of God's people. The colonial soldiers in the American Revolution often aimed for the British officers. If they killed an officer, they knew the troops under him might reel with disorganization, demoralization, and even defeat. Our adversary knows the same. Because we serve as a leader on the front lines, our adversary often aims at us. Our Lord seeks to refine us so that as we grow in holiness, we can positively impact the people under our care. These twin pressures are consistently bearing and revealing our souls to us.

Self-knowledge can be discouraging since we are not yet what we shall be (1 John 3:2). However, knowledge of self creates opportunities to grow in Christ and to be increasingly conformed to his image. This blessing extends for all of eternity.

Closing Words

Perseverance in the Ministry

To the present hour we hunger and thirst, we are poorly dressed and buffeted and homeless, and we labor, working with our own hands. When reviled, we bless; when persecuted, we endure; when slandered, we entreat. We have become, and are still, like the scum of the world, the refuse of all things.

1 Corinthians 4:11–13

Pastoral statistics are not encouraging. The Francis Schaeffer Institute of Church Leadership Development reports 35–40 percent of ministers last fewer than five years in the ministry. Many statistics show 60–80 percent of those who enter the ministry will no longer continue in the ministry ten years later.[1] Whether or not these statistics are exact, it is clear that perseverance in the ministry is a struggle.

The challenges vary. Conflict, discouragement, burnout, the cares of the world, loneliness, and moral failure often beset us. We can combat these struggles with many of the practical suggestions detailed in this book.

In this final chapter, I want to encourage you above all to persevere. Just this week I was on the phone with a pastor in another city. He currently ministers in a church racked with conflict and has endured great testing these past few weeks. His name and reputation have taken a severe hit, including false allegations lodged against him. These rumors spread not only through his church but also across segments of his denomination. People in his own church refuse to speak to him when he passes them in the hall. Unless the Lord intervenes, he clearly faces the end of his ministry at this church—a church he and his family deeply love. As we spoke on the phone he shared his thoughts about quitting ministry altogether. It's not that he no longer feels called; he is weary and tired of suffering. Ministry demands much and can be hard.

The difficulty of ministry causes too many of us to give up too soon on our calling. As I told this dear brother, the wounds are fresh, but as the Great Physician, our Lord heals. The Lord called you, dear pastor, to ministry. We dare not set aside this mantle too easily. Sometimes there are circumstances that may necessitate a break. In cases of extreme exhaustion, family concerns, or persistent struggles with particular sins, a pastor may need to leave his call. In other situations, men have been wrongly ordained, and they legitimately need to leave the pastorate. However, I would hazard to guess that many leave well before their time.

Persevere. Remember your calling. Remember that the Lord of Providence establishes every moment of your life and that he also reigns as Lord of the church. He called you. The discouragements that assail us as we try to persevere in the ministry are not an accident. They motivate growth in godliness and conformity to the image of our Suffering Savior; ultimately, our struggles work for the good of the church.

We can also be assured that many of the discouragements we face stem from the wiles and schemes of our adversary. We dare not abandon our post due to his attacks. We must persevere for the glory of God and the good of his church. By willingly submitting ourselves to suffering, we will joyfully fulfill our call in the ministry. The pastorate remains a lifelong call for most of us. Though the temptation to quit may be strong, don't give up too easily. God called you to this holiness-producing, soul-demanding, grace-manifesting, truth-telling, righteousness-pursuing, comfort-giving, love-extending, faith-building, joy-filled, and holy vocation. Persevere in it.

Suggested Reading

On Pastoring

Bonar, Horatius. *Words to Winners of Souls.* Phillipsburg, NJ: P&R, 1995.

Bridges, Charles. *The Christian Ministry: With an Inquiry into the Causes of Its Inefficiency.* 1829. Reprint, Edinburgh: Banner of Truth, 2001.

Clowney, Edmund. *Called to the Ministry.* Phillipsburg, NJ: P&R, 1964.

Piper, John. *Brothers, We Are Not Professionals: A Plea to Pastors for Radical Ministry.* Exp. ed. Nashville: B&H Books, 2013.

Still, William. *The Work of the Pastor.* Geanies House, UK: Christian Focus, 2001.

Tripp, Paul David. *Dangerous Calling: Confronting the Unique Challenges of Pastoral Ministry.* Wheaton: Crossway, 2012.

Witmer, Timothy Z. *The Shepherd Leader: Achieving Effective Shepherding in Your Church.* Phillipsburg, NJ: P&R, 2010.

On Preaching

Davis, Dale Ralph. *The Word Became Fresh: How to Preach from Old Testament Narrative Texts*. Reprint, Geanies House, UK: Christian Focus, 2007.

Ellsworth, Wilbur. *The Power of Speaking God's Word: How to Preach Memorable Sermons*. Geanies House, UK: Christian Focus, 2000.

Goldsworthy, Graeme. *Preaching the Whole Bible as Christian Scripture: The Application of Biblical Theology to Expository Preaching*. Grand Rapids: Eerdmans, 2000.

Helm, David R. *Expositional Preaching: How We Speak God's Word Today*. Wheaton: Crossway, 2014.

Lloyd-Jones, D. Martyn. *Preaching and Preachers*. 40th anniv. ed. Grand Rapids: Zondervan, 2011.

Miller, Calvin. *Preaching: The Art of Narrative Exposition*. Grand Rapids: Baker Books, 2006.

Piper, John. *The Supremacy of God in Preaching*. Rev. ed. Grand Rapids: Baker Books, 2004.

Plantinga, Cornelius, Jr. *Reading for Preaching: The Preacher in Conversation with Storytellers, Biographers, Poets, and Journalists*. Grand Rapids: Eerdmans, 2013.

On Leadership

Carson, D. A. *The Cross and Christian Ministry: Leadership Lessons from 1 Corinthians*. Grand Rapids: Baker Books, 2004.

Mohler, Albert. *The Conviction to Lead: 25 Principles for Leadership That Matters*. Minneapolis: Bethany House, 2012.

Sanders, J. Oswald. *Spiritual Leadership: A Commitment to Excellence for Every Believer*. New ed. Chicago: Moody, 2007.

On Counseling

Emlet, Michael. *Cross Talk: Where Life and Scripture Meet.* Greensboro, NC: New Growth Press, 2009.

Powlison, David. *Seeing with New Eyes: Counseling and the Human Condition through the Lens of Scripture.* Phillipsburg, NJ: P&R, 2003.

———. *Speaking Truth in Love: Counsel in Community.* Winston-Salem, NC: Punch Press, 2005.

Tripp, Paul David. *Instruments in the Redeemer's Hands: People in Need of Change Helping People in Need of Change.* Phillipsburg, NJ: P&R, 2002.

Welch, Edward T. *When People Are Big and God Is Small: Overcoming Peer Pressure, Codependency, and the Fear of Man.* Phillipsburg, NJ: P&R, 1997.

Other Helpful Resources

Carson, D. A. *Praying with Paul: A Call to Spiritual Reformation: Priorities from Paul and His Prayers.* 2nd ed. Grand Rapids: Baker Academic, 2015. Originally published in 1992 as *A Call to Spiritual Reformation: Priorities from Paul and His Prayers.*

———. *Memoirs of an Ordinary Pastor.* Wheaton: Crossway, 2008.

DeYoung, Kevin, and Greg Gilbert. *What Is the Mission of the Church? Making Sense of Social Justice, Shalom, and the Great Commission.* Wheaton: Crossway, 2011.

Lewis, Arthur T., and Henry M. Robert. *Robert's Rules Simplified.* Mineola, NY: Dover, 2006.

Marshall, Colin, and Tony Payne. *The Trellis and the Vine: The Ministry Mind-Shift That Changes Everything.* Kingsford, AU: Matthias Media, 2009.

Schultze, Quentin. *An Essential Guide to Public Speaking: Serving Your Audience with Faith, Skill, and Virtue.* Grand Rapids: Baker Books, 2006.

Strauch, Alexander. *Biblical Eldership: An Urgent Call to Restore Biblical Church Leadership.* Rev. and exp. ed. Colorado Springs: Lewis and Roth, 2003.

Thomas, Derek. *The Essential Commentaries for a Preacher's Library.* Rev. ed. Jackson, MS: First Pres Press, 2006.

Notes

Chapter 13 Personal Holiness Matters

1. Quoted in John Piper, "He Kissed the Rose and Felt the Thorn: Living and Dying in the Morning of Life," message at Desiring God 2011 Conference for Pastors, February 1, 2011, www.desiringgod.org/biographies/he-kissed-the -rose-and-felt-the-thorn-living-and-dying-in-the-morning-of-life.

Chapter 18 Trust His Means

1. Terry Johnson, *Reformed Worship: Worship That Is according to Scripture* (Greenville, SC: Reformed Academic Press, 2000).

2. Augustine, *Tractates on the Gospel of John* 80.3.

Chapter 31 Leading Meetings

1. Henry M. Robert III et al., *Robert's Rules of Order Newly Revised*, 11th ed. (Cambridge, MA: De Capo Press, 2011).

Chapter 41 Lecture Sermons

1. Richard Baxter, *The Poetical Fragments*, 4th ed. (London: W. Pickering, 1821), 35; accessed on Archive.org.

2. Jonathan Edwards, *Religious Affections* (Carlisle, PA: Banner of Truth, 1997), 44.

Closing Words: Perseverance in the Ministry

1. Richard J. Krejcir, "Statistics on Pastors: What Is Going On with the Pastors in America?," 2007, http://www.churchleadership.org/apps/articles /default.asp?articleid=42347&columnid=4545.